P9-BYV-370

UNDERSTANDING THE TIMES

and Knowing What to Do

Turning Point®

Copyright © 1991, 1997 by Turning Point.
All Rights Reserved.

ISBN 1-58119-030-1

(Persons identified as having life-controlling problems represent a composite of the author's pastoral experience, and no one individual is portrayed in this volume.)

No part of this publication may be reproduced, stored in a retrieval system, or transmitted in any form by any means, electronic, mechanical, photocopy, recording, or otherwise, without the prior written permission of the publisher except for brief quotations in critical reviews or articles.

Communications should be addressed to:

Turning Point Ministries, Inc.
P. O. Box 22127
Chattanooga, TN 37422-2127
email: jlee@chattanooga.net

Cover Design: Graphic Advertising
Layout: Louise Lee

Unless otherwise identified, Scripture quotations in this volume are from The Holy Bible, New International Version ® Copyright © 1973, 1978, 1984, International Bible Society. Used by permission of Zondervan Publishers. Other Scripture quotations marked KJV are from the King James Version of the Bible. Those identified TLB are from The Living Bible, and those identified as PHILLIPS are from the New Testament in Modern English, J. B. Phillips, translator.

Dedicated to my parents, Charles and Esther Lee. They taught me character by example.

CONTENTS

1

$\mathcal{L}$ifting the Fog

December 11, 1990, is the date of one of this nation's deadliest traffic accidents and Tennessee's worst in 20 years. This accident left 13 people dead, 51 injured, and 72 cars and trucks smashed and burning. In this chain-reaction pileup, cars and trucks continued to slam into one another for five minutes. Shortly after 9 a.m., a heavy fog had overtaken Interstate 75 about 40 miles north of Chattanooga. " 'It was terrible. People were just walking around. They didn't know what happened. They couldn't see,' said Hal Munck, director of the Bradley County Office of Emergency Preparedness" (*Chattanooga Times*, December 12, 1990, A1).

Hitting the wall of fog, drivers lost all visibility and began crashing into the wreckage which became their stopping place. The *Chattanooga Times* reported, "In one cluster, a car was crushed almost into a ball. A pickup truck was wrapped across the top of it. A station wagon was twisted around both vehicles, and a tractor trailer rig had jackknifed until it squeezed around the other three like a snake. Fire had melted all four into a small pile."

1

Fog has been the main factor in numerous deadly accidents both on land and in the air. Although we do not wish to minimize the seriousness of such accidents, there is a greater type of fog that is wrecking individuals, families, churches, and nations. The above reference to "People were just walking around. They didn't know what happened. They couldn't see," sounds much like people in our society today. Families are crashing. America and other nations are approaching the bottom, if not already there, in morals. Lives are being ripped apart, yet people do not know how or why it is happening. Simply stated, they are in a fog. This book is all about lifting the fog from our personal lives, families, and churches. Lifting the fog from ourselves and in these institutions will clear the vision so our world can get off the crash course it is on. Throughout this book, we will look at various destructive models and examples of living that create a foggy outlook and see how biblical and time-proven frameworks of life can lift the fog. Psalm 119:18 declares, "Open my eyes that I may see wonderful things in your law."

Rapid Changes

Alvin Toffler, considered by many as one of the world's best-known social thinkers, describes the changes that are taking place as the "powershift." He describes powerful corporations such as General Motors, the three television networks (ABC, CBS, NBC), and IBM as examples of the powershift. They have moved from being models far superior to their competition to operating in a survival mode.

Toffler also describes American medical doctors as examples of the powershift. In the past, medical doctors were considered gods with little resistance from their patients. "Today, by contrast, American doctors are under siege. Patients talk back. They sue for malpractice. Nurses demand responsibility and respect. Pharmaceutical companies are less deferential. . . . Insurance companies, 'managed care groups,' and government, not doctors, [are] now in control of the American health system" (Toffler, 5).

As we live with the impending change of millennia, there is a saying frequently heard, "We're living in the nineties." The nineties have pinned labels on people, the most common being baby boomers for people born between 1946 and 1964. Baby busters are those after the baby boom generation and Generation Xers are those generally known as the twenty-somethings.

The nineties can be characterized best as a time of misplaced priorities, uncertainty, and transition—to what many do not seem to know. Politicians have drawn votes on "sound bites" versus substance, many sports figures have turned to greed and drugs, and we are experiencing what has to be an all-time low in trust. Church leaders, in many instances, have betrayed trust by the misuse of funds, sexual immorality, and the pursuit of their own personal kingdoms.

It seems the old acronym JOY—Jesus first, Others second and You last—no longer applies. The nineties have taught us to place self first, others second (if it helps you), and God last (if it is convenient or fits your belief system). Take care of number one no matter what—but remember, "I am not responsible for my actions." Sound familiar? If the unborn is inconvenient, then abort the child. If young children are in the way, then buckle them in their seat belts and direct the car to the floor of the lake. Or as one mother did, leave the young children in the car in the scorching heat to draw their last breath as she parties in a motel room. Help! We are dying in sea of narcissism.

The nineties certainly strikes an astounding resemblance to the Apostle Paul's view of godlessness in the last days. "But mark this: There will be terrible times in the last days. People will be lovers of themselves, lovers of money, boastful, proud, abusive, disobedient to their parents, ungrateful, unholy, without love, unforgiving, slanderous, without self-control, brutal, not lovers of the good, treacherous, rash, conceited, lovers of pleasure rather than lovers of God" (2 Timothy 3:1-4). This passage underlies the making of most major newspaper headlines.

As we move into the third millennium, we will experience a time of global information transfer, a phenomenon known as the "information highway." According to John Naisbitt and Patricia Aburdene, "In telecommunications we are moving to a single world-wide information network, just as economically we are becoming one global marketplace. We are moving toward the capability to communicate anything to anyone, anywhere, by any form–voice, data, text, or image–at the speed of light" (6). Naisbitt and Aburdene also state, "Before the year 2000 a single optic fiber will be able to transmit 10 million conversations at the same time compared with only 3,000 in 1988" (7). This information age reminds me of the prophetic message in Daniel 12:4. "But you, Daniel, close up and seal the words of the scroll until the time of the end. Many will go here and there to increase knowledge."

Looking at Paradigms

The concept of paradigms has also become a popular word in this transition of millennia. A paradigm is an example, pattern, or model. According to Webster, a paradigm can be viewed as a "philosophical and theoretical framework of a scientific school or discipline within which theories, laws, and generalizations and the experiments performed in support of them are formulated." "Paradigms are powerful because they create the lens through which we see the world" (Covey, 32). An example of a paradigm is the thinking that all great watches had to have Swiss movements. While the Swiss held steadfast to this thinking, the Japanese made quartz movements and overtook the entire watch industry.

Stephen R. Covey in his book, *The Seven Habits of Highly Effective People*, examines different kinds of paradigms. He says "paradigms are inseparable from character. Being is seeing in the human dimension. And what we see is highly interrelated to what we are. We can't go very far to change our seeing without simultaneously changing our being, and vice versa" (32). To change our paradigm, we really have to change on the inside. Jesus says, "For from within, out of men's hearts, come evil thoughts, sexual immorality, theft, murder, adultery, greed, malice, deceit, lewdness, envy, slander, arrogance and folly. All these evils come from inside and make a man 'unclean' " (Mark 7:21-23).

I had a professor in college say to me kindly more than one time, "I don't want to expose your ignorance; however, . . ." I now understand he was helping me see my faulty frame of reference which was camouflaged by my pride. He helped me start learning God's Word on a new level by first taking an inside look at the thinking patterns I established for myself. To change my basic thinking was actually a paradigm shift, a concept introduced by Thomas S. Kuhn, author of *The Structure of Scientific Revolutions.*

A framework of thought in the nineties is the popular cliché, "What you are in private has nothing to do with your public life and the two should not be mixed." This framework will crumble because what we are on the inside we will become in public. With time, it will happen.

A society and church in the Bible that clearly show a paradigm of similar dysfunction were the Corinthians and the church at Corinth. Having many of the same problems and attitudes, that society and church closely resemble our present society and church world.

The term, "We're living in the nineties," has become a popular way for many to rationalize their sin. This phrase is being used to condone so-called sexual freedom which ranges from living together without being married to homosexual lifestyles. I have even heard Christians scolded regarding their stand for righteousness with the response, "You need to get with it; we are living in the nineties." This frame of reference is the "nineties paradigm."

The Apostle Paul was faced with similar thinking which seems to have been a common saying in the Corinthian society. In 1 Corinthians 6:12b, he said: " 'Everything is permissible for me'—but I will not be mastered by anything." The Corinthian society was known to be affluent and paganistic, and their godless lifestyles were having an influence on the church. In the Corinthian church there were factions, lawsuits among believers in pagan courts, immorality, incest between a member of the church and his stepmother, jealousy, quarreling, and the misuse of the Lord's Supper and spiritual gifts. Therefore, Paul issued a personal response in 1 Corinthians 6:12, ". . . I will not be mastered by anything." In today's society that response would sound like this: "Although anything goes (we're living in the nineties), I will not be addicted to anything [or anyone]."

There are numerous frames of reference that can be described as a paradigm. A life-controlling issue, an addiction, or whatever term you choose to call a "mastery" problem is a paradigm. An addiction is bound by certain patterns and laws. Other areas of life have paradigms including traditions, doctrines, prejudices, and so forth. Each church denomination and congregation thinks and acts within a paradigm and often has a collection of paradigms within each body. For example, it is difficult to bring about change for the good if a church or an element in the body is stuck in a prejudiced way of thinking. Also, family units, both functional and dysfunctional, have their own behaviors which are handed down through each generation. These handed-down behaviors create set patterns of living from family to family.

The purpose of this book is to help you take a look at various examples of models that are constructive for living a godly life and models of dysfunction that lead to destruction, pain, and suffering. Sometimes a paradigm change is needed to survive, adjust, or improve.

> A paradigm, in a sense, tells you that there is a game, what the game is, and how to play it successfully. The idea of a game is a very appropriate metaphor for paradigms because it reflects the need for borders and directions on how to perform correctly. A paradigm tells you how to play the game according to the rules. A paradigm shift, then, is a change to a new game, a new set of rules (Barker, 37).

We have become an addictive society, and in this type of social environment there are many traps. As you read this book, be open to the Lord's direction. If a change is needed, He will help you. He has the perfect plan for your life. His rules never change and His love never fails. Although we are living in a world of rapid change, God's schedule remains the same.

2

$\mathcal{T}$he Trap

John and Becky are 50-year-olds who attend church every Sunday and on Wednesday evenings. To look at them on Sunday morning, it would seem they are a happy Christian couple; however, the police know their address very well. During the last two years, they have become regular visitors to this home.

There are two life-controlling problems in this home. John has uncontrolled anger, and Becky, though frequently physically and verbally abused, covers for his violent behavior because she believes it is the "Christian thing" to do. This violent behavior and unhealthy cover-up have gradually worsened over the years. John, who was abused by his father when he was a child, has been abusing his wife for years, but it has escalated to the point where her wounds can no longer be covered up.

These mastering problems have not only trapped John and Becky, but because they have been covered up and not dealt with, their children have also been caught in this web of pain.

A life-controlling problem is anything that masters (or controls) a person's life. Many terms have been used to describe life-controlling problems. Someone may speak of a "dependency," a "compulsive behavior," or an "addiction." In 2 Corinthians 10:4, the Apostle Paul uses the word stronghold to describe an area of sin that has become a part of our lifestyle when he writes that there is "divine power to demolish strongholds."

The easiest life-controlling problems to identify are harmful habits like drug or alcohol use, eating disorders, sexual addictions, gambling, tobacco use, and the like. Life-controlling problems can also include harmful feelings like anger and fear. The word addiction or dependency can refer to the use of a substance (like food, alcohol, legal and/or illegal drugs, etc.,), or it can refer to the practice of a behavior (like shoplifting, gambling, use of pornography, compulsive spending, TV watching, etc.). It can also involve a relationship with another person. We call those relationships "co-dependencies."

The Apostle Paul talks about life-controlling problems in terms of our being "slaves" to this behavior or dependency that masters us. He writes in Romans 6:14, "Sin shall not be your master." In 1 Corinthians 6:12b, he says, " 'Everything is permissible for me'—but I will not be mastered by anything [or anyone]."

According to 2 Peter 2:19b, "A man is a slave to whatever has mastered him." Anything that becomes the center of a person's life—if allowed to continue—will become master of that life. Because we live in a world today that can be described as an addictive society, most people are affected in some way by a life-controlling problem—their own or someone else's.

Everyone has the potential of being mastered by a life-controlling problem. No one plans for it to happen, but—without warning—an individual (and those who care about him) can be pulled into the downward spiral of a stronghold.

Addictions and Idols

Idolatry leads to addiction. When we follow idols, a choice has been made to look to a substance, behavior, or relationship for solutions that can be provided only by God. We have a *felt need* to serve a supreme being; if we choose not to serve God, we will choose an idol to which we will become enslaved. Jeffrey VanVonderen says:

> Anything besides God to which we turn, positive or negative, in order to find life, value, and meaning is idolatry: money, property, jewels, sex, clothes, church buildings, educational degrees, anything! Because of Christ's performance on the cross, life, value, and purpose are available to us in gift form only. Anything we do, positive or negative, to earn that which is life by our own performance is idolatrous: robbing a bank, cheating on our spouse, people-pleasing, swindling our employer, attending church, giving 10 percent, playing the organ for twenty years, anything (16)!

Following idols, which leads to addictions, prevents us from serving and loving God freely. All kinds of substance and behavioral dependencies lead to enslavement because everyone who makes sinful choices is a candidate for slavery to sin (*see* John 8.34). Jesus states in John 8:32 that "the truth will set you free." God spoke to Moses in Exodus 20:3, "You shall have no other gods before me." Sin, when unconfessed, strains the relationship with God that is meant to be enjoyed by the believer (*see* Proverbs 28:13; Jonah 2:8).

A very controversial question arises: Is an addiction a sin or a disease? Those who believe addictions are sin point to the acts of the sinful nature which include a substance (drunkenness) and behavioral (sexual immorality) problem in Galatians 5:19-21. Another reference to the sinfulness of addictions is 1 Corinthians 6:9-11 which shows that a definite change occurred in the lives of the Corinthian Christians: "And that is what some of you were. But you were washed, you were sanctified, you were justified in the name of the Lord Jesus Christ and by the Spirit of our God."

Those who believe addictions (particularly alcoholism and other chemical dependencies) are a disease state the characteristics are progressive, primary, chronic, and fatal. In the latter stages, the victims are incapable of helping themselves because there is a loss of control and choice. "In the 1950s the American Medical Association voted approval of the disease concept of alcohol depen-

dence. The term disease means 'deviation from a state of health' "
(Minirth, 57).

When sin and addiction are compared, they show similar characteristics. Both are self-centered versus God-centered and cause
people to live in a state of deception. Sin and addiction lead people
to irresponsible behavior, including the use of various defenses to
cover up their ungodly actions. Sin and addiction are progressive;
people get worse if there is not an intervention. Jesus healed the
man at the pool of Bethesda and later saw him at the temple. Jesus
warned him about the progressiveness of sin: "See, you are well
again. Stop sinning or something worse may happen to you" (John
5:14). Sin is primary in that it is the root cause of evil. Sin produces
sinners as alcohol causes alcoholism. Sin is also chronic if not dealt
with effectively. Finally, sin is fatal with death being the end result.

Although addictions do have the characteristics of a disease, I
must stand with the authority of God's Word as it pronounces various addictions as being a part of the sinful nature (see 1
Corinthians 6:9-11; Galatians 5:19-21). They are sinful because God
has been voided as the source of the solution to life's needs, and
these choices often develop into a disease. A noted Christian psychiatrist says:

> Physiologically, of course, some people are more prone to alco-
> holism than others, even after one drink. And often guilt drives
> them to more and more drinking. But then some people also have
> more of a struggle with greed, lust, smoking, anger, or overeating
> than others. Failure to contend with all of these is still sin (Minirth,
> 57-58).

Anything that becomes the center of one's life, if allowed to continue, will become the master of life. If God is not the center of a
person's life, that person will probably turn to a substance, behavior, or another person for focus and meaning. David describes his
enemy in Psalm 52 as one "who did not make God his stronghold
but trusted in his great wealth and grew strong by destroying others"
(v7).

The young, rich ruler described in the gospels (*see* Matthew

19:16-29; Mark 10:17-30; Luke 18:18-30) came to Jesus asking how to receive eternal life. When Jesus told him he would have to sell everything he had, give it to the poor, and follow him, the young man went away sad. This rich man's stronghold was the love of money. Everybody, not only the rich, must guard against this "greater love" of the rich young man. Paul writes: "People who want to get rich fall into temptation and a trap and into many foolish and harmful desires that plunge men into ruin and destruction. For the love of money is a root of all kinds of evil. Some people, eager for money, have wandered from the faith and pierced themselves with many griefs" (1 Timothy 6:9-10).

This stronghold, the love of money, is the root cause of most addictions that plague our society. Although alcohol is a major cause of deaths, sicknesses, broken families, and relationships, it continues to be advertised with marketing strategies which appeal even to America's high school and elementary-aged children. The demand for cocaine and other substances would soon cease if there were no profits to be made. Sexual addictions are fed by an $8 billion industry of pornographic materials, appealing television commercials, and provocative movies. Compulsive gambling is fed by state-run lotteries. I wonder how much the love of money contributes to eating disorders. Many young women starve themselves to sickness and even death because of a greedy society that promotes an unhealthy thinness as beauty through media appeal and modeling agencies.

As the creation of God, each of us has a need to be dependent. There is a vacuum in the heart of every human since the fall of Adam and Eve that can be filled only by Christ. After our first parents disobeyed God, they immediately recognized their nakedness. Without God's covering, they hid themselves "from the LORD God among the trees of the garden" (Genesis 3:8). They soon learned they could not escape from God.

Where can I go from your Spirit?
Where can I flee from your presence?
If I go up to the heavens, you are there;

if I make my bed in the depths, you are there (Psalm 139:7-8).

It is interesting that Adam and Eve hid among the trees. They hid there because of guilt. Idols, which are false gods, can also become hiding places. Isaiah writes: "for we have made a lie our refuge and falsehood [or false gods] our hiding place" (28:15).

In a life where Christ is not the focus, a person is likely to center attention on a substance, behavior, or another person which will eventually become a god to them. David recognized the need to have God as his tower of strength.

> The LORD is my rock, my fortress and my deliverer;
> my God is my rock, in whom I take refuge,
> my shield and the horn of my salvation.
> He is my stronghold, my refuge and my savior—
> from violent men you save me (2 Samuel 22:2-3).

The disease concept of addictions should be approached with caution. Assigning addictive substances and behaviors to the disease model tends to overlook the sinful nature of mankind. Although it is popular to label every stronghold as a disease, the Church must warmly care for those caught in the web of deception with ongoing support. It takes more than a pat on the back to cure them of their stronghold. Sinful choices develop into lifestyles that are self-centered and destructive. The fall of man puts us all in need of recovery.

How the Trap Works

Addictions and dependencies generally fall into three categories: substance addictions, behavior addictions, and relationship (interaction) addictions.

1. **Substance addictions** (the use of substances taking control of our lives)
   • Drugs/chemicals

- Food (eating disorders)
- Alcohol
- Other addictive substances

2. **Behavior addictions** (the practice of behaviors taking control of our lives)
   - Gambling
   - Compulsive spending
   - Use of pornography/other sexual addiction
   - Love of money
   - Sports
   - Other addictive behavior

3. **Relationship (interaction) addictions** (You may have heard a relationship problem like this referred to as "co-dependency.") This is discussed in more detail in Chapter 8.

Everyone has the potential of experiencing one or more of these life-controlling problems at some time. Maybe you find yourself already involved in an addiction or another problem behavior that has taken over your life. Sometimes it is hard to identify a life-controlling problem. Here are some questions that may help in that process:
1. Is my behavior practiced in secret?
2. Can it meet the test of openness—or do I hide it from family and friends?
3. Does this behavior pull me away from my commitment to Christ?
4. Does it express Christian love?
5. Is this behavior used to escape feelings?
6. Does this behavior have a negative effect on myself or others?

These questions help us identify problems that have reached (or are in danger of reaching) the point of becoming life-controlling problems.

The next step is to look at the ways these behaviors and dependencies tend to progress in a person's life. Researchers have identified a pattern that follows some very predictable steps. Most people get involved with an addiction to receive a feeling of euphoria. Alcohol or other drugs, sex, pornographic literature, gambling, and so forth, produce a temporary high or euphoria.

Vernon E. Johnson, the founder and president emeritus of the Johnson Institute in Minneapolis, has observed (without trying to prove any theory) "literally thousands of alcoholics, their families, and other people surrounding them . . . we came up with the discovery that alcoholics showed certain specific conditions with a remarkable consistency" (8). Dr. Johnson uses a feeling chart to illustrate how alcoholism follows an emotional pattern. He identifies four phases: (1) learns mood swing, (2) seeks mood swing, (3) harmful dependency, (4) using to feel normal. Many of the observations made by Dr. Johnson and others, including myself, can also be related to other types of dependencies although the terminology may differ.

We call it the "Trap" because it often snares its victims before they realize what is really happening. Every person has the potential of experiencing a life-controlling problem. No one is automatically exempt. Even though no one plans to be trapped by such a problem, it can happen without a person's even being aware.

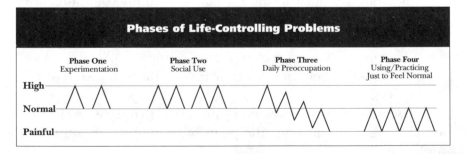

Figure 2-1

Phases of Life-Controlling Problems

Phase One: **Experimentation**

- I learn that experimenting with the substance/behavior makes me feel good.
- I don't really see any serious negative consequences.
- I learn to trust the substance/behavior—to make me feel good or help me escape every time I use it or do it.
- I learn how to use the substance/behavior to make myself feel great.

Phase Two: **Social Use**

- I begin to use or practice more regularly.
- This behavior or substance becomes a part of my social life.
- I use or practice in times and places that are socially acceptable.
- Daily lifestyle choices begin to be affected by my focus on this substance/behavior.
- I make rules for myself about my use/practice to make me feel "safe."
- My use/behavior becomes a problem without warning.

Phase Three: **Daily Preoccupation**

- My use/practice becomes a harmful dependency.
- I begin to lose control over my use/practice.
- I violate my value system.
- I cannot block out the emotional pain.
- My lifestyle is centered on this compulsive behavior.
- Unresolved problems produce more stress and pain.
- I break my self-imposed "safe use/practice" rules.
- My life deteriorates in all areas, including health, spirituality, and relationships.

Phase Four: **Using/Practicing Just to Feel Normal**

- I lose touch with reality and experience delusions and paranoia.
- I may try to escape my problems by running away.
- I lose my desire to live.
- I have no desire for God—I am spiritually bankrupt.
- I lose control and dignity.
- My problems grow in a "snowball" effect.
- My family relationships are destroyed (Lee, 1995, 22-23).

Biblical Examples

Genesis 4 records the account of Cain and a problem that mastered his life. He and his brother, Abel, brought their offerings to the Lord. Abel's offering was accepted, but Cain's fruits of the ground were not received by the Lord. Cain became very angry, and his face displayed his feelings. The Lord saw his anger and facial expressions and encouraged him to do what was right so that his offering and he would be accepted.

The Lord followed with a statement which illustrates how problems can become our master. "But if you do not do what is right, sin is crouching at your door; it desires to have you, but you must master it" (Genesis 4:7). The Lord recognized a potential life-controlling problem crouching and ready to pounce on Cain if he opened the door. Cain opened the door, and anger became his master. He invited Abel to the field and killed him. When the Lord asked where Abel was, Cain responded trying to cover his evil actions by denying any knowledge of his brother's whereabouts.

Allowing anger to rule his life, Cain committed murder, became a restless wanderer, and went from the presence of the Lord, thus alienating himself from God. Fed by jealousy, rebellion, and unbelief, anger became a stronghold in his life. This is an example of a life-controlling problem that is permitted to continue without intervention.

The concept of life-controlling stages is addressed in James 1:14-15: "but each one is tempted when, by his own evil desire, he is dragged away and enticed. Then, after desire has conceived, it gives birth to sin; and sin, when it is full-grown, gives birth to death." The downward spiral starts with *temptation* (an attraction to). The second stage is *desire* (to long for). Desire conceives and gives birth to the third stage, *sin*. The final stage is *death*.

James' concept of life-controlling problems can be compared with a marriage to an addiction. The marriage begins with *courtship*. Although initially the victim may not recognize the courtship as such because it is appealing, he/she is tempted and drawn to an addiction. The person is enticed and lured into a relationship and gives *consent,* and an addiction takes hold with a *conception* of a problem that now starts to master a person's life.

Months or even years later, there is the birth of a *child* (trouble). The fruit of the life-controlling problem causes all kinds of problems in the home, church, school, and workplace. The relationship arrives at a place of *completion*. In this stage, the marriage has become fatalistic (destructive relationship) to the victim and has hurt those who are close. The end result is *corruption*. If the relationship is not broken with the addiction, death always follows: spiritual, emotional, and physical.

There are certain stages involved in David's sin with Bathsheba as recorded in 2 Samuel 11. In stage one, "From the roof he saw a woman bathing" (v2). David entered stage two when he "sent someone to find out about her" (v3). In the third stage, "David sent messengers to get her. She came to him, and he slept with her" (v4). To further complicate matters, David tried to cover up his sin which led to the murder of Bathsheba's husband.

Joshua 7 discusses Achan's sin of disobedience which led to his death. After the Lord delivered Jericho into the hands of Joshua and the Israelites, they were commanded to stay away from the sacred things which included "all the silver and gold and the articles of bronze and iron" (6:19). Achan's sin was a violation of this command and was committed in stages. In the first stage he "saw in the plunder a beautiful robe from Babylonia, two hundred shekels of silver and a wedge of gold weighing fifty shekels" (7:21). Achan followed his temptation by coveting the riches (stage two). Then, he took the riches (stage three) and hid them. In addition to his own death, his sin adversely affected the entire nation of Israel just as life-controlling problems often go beyond the victim's hurting only himself.

As a rule with few exceptions, life-controlling problems do not occur overnight. I have met with parents who have tragically lost a child to chemical dependency. Many times they wanted to think the child had just started using drugs. There was the wife who caught her husband entertaining a prostitute, and she believed his insistence that this was the first time. Actually, for those who have reached the ultimate end of their addiction, whether physical death or emotional and spiritual death, their death occurred on the installment plan. They died one phase at a time. Paul writes: "For the wages of sin is death, but the gift of God is eternal life in Christ Jesus our Lord" (Romans 6:23).

On the way from my motel to the airport in Oklahoma City, the taxi driver explained how his life had been totally destroyed by gambling. Not knowing that his passenger had just taught the phases of a life-controlling problems at a seminar, he proceeded to tell me how phase by phase he became controlled by gambling. At one time the head of a corporation with a salary in six figures, he started experimenting by playing the state lottery. Gambling became a social part of his life in which he bet on various sporting events. The infrequent big wins kept him coming back for a larger win. Gambling became the center of his life and progressed to become his one and only master. He not only lost his position and dignity but his family as well. In the ten-minute ride to the airport, he explained in detail the process I had just taught.

3

$\mathcal{W}$hy We Are an Addictive Society

While watching a baseball play-off game, I was amazed when the announcers chastised the owner of one of the teams. They complained that she would not renew the contract of the manager for the next year because at the time, he was living with a woman and the couple was not married. The national network announcers reminded the audience that this behavior was okay in today's society. It is the accepted thing. This is contemporary America. They were proclaiming the nineties theme, "We're living in the nineties."

Moral Base Erosion

We have become an addictive society because the moral base has eroded. "There is absolutely no moral consensus at all in the 1990s. Everyone is making up their own personal moral codes—their own Ten Commandments" (Patterson and Kim, 25). Israel experienced a time when everyone followed his own moral code without regard for others. "In those days Israel had no king; everyone did as he saw fit" (Judges 21:25). Selfishness is the very root of this mind-set.

19

James Patterson and Peter Kim also report in their book, *The Day America Told the Truth*, that only "one in ten of us [Americans] believes in all of the Ten Commandments" (200). They further report that about one-fourth of us believes in witchcraft (28%), black magic (24%), and voodoo (20%) (204). When we refuse to acknowledge almighty God, we become our own god. The first commandment says, "You shall have no other gods before me" (Exodus 20:3).

The real issue in the "prayer in schools" debate is not prayer. No government power can stop a student from praying. For those who want to pray, no one can stop them; therefore, the issue is recognition of Almighty God. It seems that taking God's name in vain is acceptable—God is seen as a bad word. Since America no longer has a Judeo-Christian value system, thousands and thousands of children are growing up with no respect for God because He is neither acknowledged in the home nor at school. It is not surprising that as we make this millennium transition, the growth of social ills such as drugs, crime, teenage pregnancy, abortion, and so forth, are directly related to the lack of respect for God. Without this respect for the Almighty, we have no rules or a plan for the game of life. Therefore, society develops its own rules, and because they are not founded in truth, these rules always change and keep us confused.

Media Influence

As I worked a drug prevention program in public high schools a few years ago, I was surprised to hear the conversation of rural area students very similar to the conversation of urban area students. How could this be? What was the common link? The link I found was the media. The media portrayal of illicit sex, drugs, violence, and the mockery of traditional family values is contributing much to our addictive society. George Barna reports in his book, *Absolute Confusion*:

> According to the American people, one of the big winners in the repositioning of influences has been the mass media. Six out of ten

respondents told us that journalists and media personalities have more influence today than they did 5 years ago; only 1 out of every eight respondents said the media have less influence these days . . . Among the boomers and busters, the influence of the media was said to have increased rather than decreased by better than an 8 to 1 margin (26).

On November 27, 1995, in the *Chattanooga Free Press,* an Associated Press writer reported:

New York—In a virtual replay of scenes from the new movie Money Train, two men squeezed a flammable liquid into a subway token booth and ignited it, blowing it up and critically burning the clerk. 'We know from experience that when you get movie and television depictions of criminal activity, it is often copycatted,' Transit Authority President Alan Kiepper said after the explosion Sunday.

One of the best publications on the media's influence is *Youth and Drugs: Society's Mixed Message* published by the U.S. Department of Health and Human Services. In this publication, Todd Gitlin, Ph.D., says, "By their nature, the media reflect that culture [consumer-oriented thrill seeking] and have conditioned Americans to accept drug use as part of it" (Resnik, 31). Other significant points in this book include: "In important ways, television, more than the other mass media, can be likened to a drug and the audience's dependency on it to a kind of addiction. . . . For many people, television is a dulling, low-risk sort of drug. Many people, especially children, watch it in sort of a trance" (Resnik, 39). Television can be experienced as both a stimulant and a depressant. Like ingested drugs, it is often combined with food or conversation. Viewers say it makes them feel "drowsy," "weak," and "passive" (Resnik, 39). People tend to turn to television when in personal difficulties and to binge on it (Resnik, 39). Chuck Colson in his book, *The Body,* says, "While Scripture provided the most cohesive force in culture forty years ago, it seems that the base of common understanding and communication today is the television networks" (167).

There is no question that television elevates pleasure and in doing so contributes heavily to this addictive society. It places a thirst in the individual to pursue pleasure without counting the cost. It is no surprise then that to abstain from television is to suffer withdrawal symptoms such as depression, insomnia, and chain-smoking (Resnik, 39).

Poor Adult Guidance

As the saying goes, "values are best caught, not taught." Of course, parents should be the most positive influence on their children. It is my view that extremely active church youth groups and school groups that do not work in partnership with the parents can hinder the influence of parents on their children. Since adults generally have more experience and maturity, their influence is far more important than peer influence. However, if youth spend more time with their peers than they do with their parents, it is obvious who will have the most influence. It is a mistake to expect the church to take on the role of the parent thereby excusing the parents of their responsibility of time. It is healthy for church youth groups to have activities with the parents.

There are exceptions. Many youth do not have the benefit of responsible parents, so in this case the church can serve in the parenting role. Generally speaking though, the role of the church youth group is to lend support to the parents and not be in competition with them.

It is important to examine adult-youth relationships. Having fun with teenagers is enjoyable and great; however, the adult to youth relationship should not become confusing. A youth leader who tries to be cool and act like the gang is probably ineffective. To the leader's face, his actions may seem to be met with approval, but inside, the youth are probably laughing at the leader's immaturity. Also, at no time should youth leaders probe into the sexual life of a teenager. Many well-meaning youth pastors have fallen prey to this trap.

Adult guidance should challenge youth. I know this is not popular in our addictive society. I remember starting a drug prevention program a few years ago in a high school. In preparation for a sign-up to the newly formed Triple S (Students Staying Straight) group, every student in the school was talked to in classroom presentations about making a commitment to abstain from drug and alcohol use. By signing to be a member of the group, he or she would be making a commitment to abstain from drugs and alcohol for that school year.

Prior to the scheduled sign-up on Monday morning, I met with the school counselor and a teacher to prepare for the event. The teacher scolded me by saying, "Who are you to ask these students not to drink? You are imposing your values on them. You will be lucky if 25 students sign up." I left the meeting very discouraged but with a clear picture of how adults who are unwilling to challenge youth are actually contributing to our addictive society.

During the second period class on Monday, the principal made an announcement about the sign-up saying, "Any student wishing to join the Triple S Club, please go immediately to the cafeteria." After the announcement, I was tense with the silence in the halls; then boom—it happened. The students flooded the hallways, and the cafeteria was not large enough to hold the number of students who came to sign up. Once again I learned an important lesson: youth want to be challenged.

It is interesting to note that later in the school year a young lady who was one of the top students in the senior class told the school counselor she must talk with me and implied urgency. After the counselor called, I rushed to the school expecting the worse, but her words to me were, "Mr. Lee, I was offered drugs this week, and I turned them down."

There is much talk today about the distribution of condoms in schools to prevent sexually transmitted diseases. "Oh, yes," the proponents of this "think tank" will say, "we want students to abstain from sex until they are mature; however, if they can't, let's provide them a condom for protection." That statement is a contribution to the problem. It is my view that many adults make these statements because they do not abstain from immorality, so they feel uncomfortable in asking the youth to refrain from sex outside marriage.

Breakdown of Community

As we move into the third millennium, the individual is being exalted above the community. Talk, talk, talk. Talk radio and TV talk show ratings seem to explode on individual rights (with little being said about responsibility), meism, mid-life crisis, one night affairs, and so forth. When a society exists on what it can get by with legally, it ceases to be community. Instead, selfish individualism leads to isolation. We will discuss isolation in Chapter 5. "We don't know our neighbors. . . . The great majority of Americans (72 percent) openly admit that they don't know the people next door." (Patterson and Kim, 172). It is okay "to stand on your own two feet" as an individual, but one must always be aware of his need for God and others. The body of believers is a community designed to be in a relationship with Christ and one another in the body of Christ.

The late President John F. Kennedy's popular words, "Ask not what your country can do for you, ask what you can do for your country," can also be applied to relationships. Substitute the word country for wife, husband, family, business, church, and friends. If we practice this in the spirit of Christ, we will see the healing of relationships beyond our wildest imagination. Unfortunately, many relationships, including marriage, are only to satisfy one's own needs with little concern for the other person.

> It is not surprising therefore that we view people and society as "things" to be "used" for our individual satisfaction and growth. It goes without question that the individual predominates over the group. This mentality threads through our approach to all strata of relationship building. . . . Friendship today is viewed as important for meeting "my personal needs" (Gorman, 57).

Another factor influencing the breakdown of community is our technology. Instead of a nice, friendly voice answering the telephone, we now have voice mail that sends us on endless trails. Many people in the workplace are no more than a number on the computer screen as they sit at their desks. We have more and more conveniences with our advanced technology but less time for one another. The "information highway" connects people with information but does not fulfill personal community.

The breakdown of community is highly motivated by the profit margin. In order to stay in business, retail merchants of all sorts have cut services once performed by people who built relationships and cared for their customers. All these factors are a part of doing business, so we have to work at restoring community even more. Hopefully, a time will come when the public will demand a return to service.

Although sometimes necessary, the mobility of people contributes to the breakdown of community. This can be disruptive and often devastating on families. "People's lives are in a constant state of flux. In the past five years, more than one out of four adults has changed churches; nearly four out of ten have changed their address; most people in the labor pool have changed jobs; and half now live at a different financial level than they did in 1987" (Barna, 105). All this lack of community shows the great potential for the church as a Christ-centered, caring community to be a force as we move into the next millennium.

Enabling: Helping or Hurting

We contribute to an addictive society when we continue to help people although they abuse our help. The enabler becomes a part of the problem. Enabling is one of the threads that holds an addictive society together. Enablers include parents, governments, schools, teachers, physicians, lawyers, clergy, and so forth.

Raymond's parents tried over and over again to help him with his drug use. By age 12, he started drinking at a friend's house on the weekend and was dependent on alcohol and other drugs by age 15. He was raised by Christian parents, and they attended church regularly. At age 21, Raymond's life was a wreck. His drug use resulted in his killing a very close family friend and serving a lengthy prison sentence.

During Raymond's teenage years, his parents contributed to his drug use although they thought they were helping. They changed churches several times because Raymond did not like the church, or when he was corrected by a Sunday school teacher, the parents would always side with Raymond.

Mr. Polk, the high school principal, called Raymond's mother on a Friday in the fall of the year. He had suspected for some time that Raymond was selling marijuana on school property, but this time he knew for sure because a teacher monitoring the grounds during lunch saw him sell the substance to another student. Having received the news concerning Raymond, his mother became angry and blamed Mr. Polk and his staff for a poorly run school. She threatened to bring a lawsuit against him and the high school for bringing such an accusation against Raymond. In the conference with the principal and the teacher who caught Raymond with marijuana in his possession, the parents sided with Raymond and gave a tongue lashing to the school officials. They transferred their son to a private Christian school, but Raymond's behavior and his parents' way of dealing with his problem did not change.

During the course of one year, Raymond was arrested five times for driving under the influence of alcohol. Each time his parents bailed him out of jail giving him "one more chance" thinking they were helping him. They built their life around Raymond covering up for his deviant behavior. The other children were neglected. Three days before Raymond's eighteenth birthday, the marriage of the parents ended. Their kind of "helping" had turned into pain for the entire family.

Charles and Lois were Christian parents who had a 17-year-old son addicted to chemicals. Lois called Max, the director of a Christian drug treatment program in their city, and asked for an appointment to discuss their son's problem. At the meeting, Max gave the parents a book to give to their son, Bill. Max agreed to visit with their son the next day. Charles and Lois went home and gave the book to Bill, and he agreed to meet with Max as scheduled.

The next day, a snowy day in February, Max drove up to Bill's house. He felt the strain immediately as he entered the home. It was apparent the son had drained them financially, emotionally, and spiritually. Lois greeted Max at the door and said, "Bill is in his bedroom and and he doesn't want to see you." Bill was permitted to control entry into his bedroom. Although it was against his parents' wishes, he used drugs in his room without their successful intervention.

Observing the pain on Lois's face, Max commented, "If it's okay with you, I will go in and see Bill anyway." It seemed to be a relief to Lois that a person would actually violate Bill's privacy. Max knocked on Bill's door and said, "I want to talk with you, Bill." When there was no response, Max gently opened the door and found Bill lying on his bed hallucinating from a chemical. Max felt uneasy, but he sat down on the corner of Bill's bed and said, "Bill, what are you on?" Bill responded by handing him a folded piece of paper. Max's first thought was "Oh, it's LSD." He opened the paper and was surprised to see a ten-dollar bill. Moving in and out of reality and euphoria, Bill said with tears in his eyes, "This is my last ten dollars from selling drugs at Central High School [he had dropped out four months earlier], and it's for your program." Max then noticed a written message with the money. The note said: I NEED GOD'S LOVE MORE THAN DRUGS. YET I'M CONFUSED. I FEEL USED, I WANT OFF THE MERRY-GO-ROUND OF DRUGS. Bill went into Max's program and had a remarkable recovery.

Bill's loving parents were doing what they thought was right, but permitting Bill to have privacy and use chemicals in his bedroom was hurting instead of helping. Actually, Bill wanted Max to enter the bedroom without an invitation.

Enabling and Rescuing Behaviors

There is a word that is used to describe the actions of people such as the parents of Raymond and Bill: *enabling*. Although there are many good uses of this word, in our context it is a negative term. Enabling is anything that stands in the way of or softens the natural consequences of a person's behavior. Although they were loving parents, they stood in the way of the consequences of their children's behavior. Raymond's parents continually rescued him from the consequences of his deviant behavior. Charles and Lois permitted Bill to use drugs in their home thereby harming a person they loved very much.

Unknowingly, an enabler helps the one he cares for to continue the downward spiral of addiction. He continues to help even though his assistance is being abused. Another term used for enabling is rescuing. The writer of Proverbs states: "A hot-tempered man must pay the penalty; if you rescue him, you will have to do it again" (19:19).

Helpers learn to rescue their friend or loved one from responsibilities. "As counselor Scott Egleston says, we rescue anytime we take responsibility for another human being—for that person's thoughts, feelings, decisions, behaviors, growth, well-being, problems, or destiny" (Beattie, 78).

Robert and Gayle were concerned about their son Eric. Being leaders in their church, they were dismayed their son would even consider drinking since he had been raised in the church. However, Eric had gotten involved with friends at school who were a bad influence. Robert began to find beer cans in his son's car and noticed a change in Eric's attitude.

As hurting parents, they visited with Joseph, a Christian counselor. Joseph encouraged them to maintain their house rules which meant Eric was required to obey curfew and not drink alcohol in their home.

After meeting with Joseph, they had a talk with Eric. They shared with him that they loved him very much, but he would be expected to follow their house rules. Eric made the decision to leave home rather than follow their rules. As he stayed away for months, Robert and Gayle pondered their decision wondering if he would be gone forever. Trusting God to bring him back, they prayed for his safety.

On a Sunday night several months after Eric made the decision to leave home, Robert and Gayle returned home from church and were pleasantly surprised to see that Eric had come back. He was in bed and had left a personal letter for his parents.

> I know I'm the last person on this earth that should ask you for help after all you've done for me, but I really need help from y'all right now. I know it seems strange writing you a letter, but I really don't

know if I know how to talk to you this serious face-to-face. I guess the bottom line is I'm hooked on drugs and alcohol and need help (counseling?) to straighten myself up before it's too late. . . . I'd be so thankful. Any extra expenses that come out of this ordeal are fully understood to be taken care of by me and the sooner the better. If I can't change my ways now, I know I can never amount to anything. I love you very much and don't ever want to hurt you or myself anymore.

Love, your son,

Eric

Robert called Joseph and set up an appointment for Eric, himself, and his wife. Eric was serious in his commitment to change and entered into a Christian rehabilitation program that dealt with life-controlling problems. His life was changed, and his family was reunited.

Although they loved him very much, Robert and Gayle did not enable Eric. They did not loosen the standards of their home, nor did they try to rescue Eric after he made the decision to leave home. This was difficult for them as loving parents because they knew he had a trail of problems following him.

Biblical Examples

The enabling behaviors of Jezebel are recorded in 1 Kings 21. Her husband, King Ahab, became angry and pouted because Naboth would not sell him his vineyard. When Jezebel noticed Ahab and his sullen condition, she devised a deceitful plan to get the vineyard for him and rescue him from his pouting spell.

Using the official seal, she wrote letters in her husband's name declaring a day of fasting. She placed Naboth in a prominent position and had two scoundrels testify against him saying he was guilty of cursing God and King Ahab. Jezebel's enabling behavior led to the death of Naboth. The writer of 1 Kings describes Jezebel as a person who urged Ahab to do evil (*see* 21:25).

The prodigal son chose to take his part of the inheritance and leave home (*see* Luke 15:11-32). He went to a distant country and wasted his wealth. Having run out of money, he worked in a citizen's field feeding pigs. He finally came to his senses or broke out of his delusion and said: "I will set out and go back to my father and say to him: Father, I have sinned against heaven and against you" (v18). His father welcomed him home with acceptance and compassionate love.

The father exhibited characteristics of a person who helps instead of hurts. Although it was painful to see his son leave, the father did not attempt to rescue him from the decision he made. Luke writes in verse 16: " . . . but no one gave him anything." The father helped his son break out of delusion by not enabling him. When the son recognized his sin and confessed it, he received mercy from his father. The prodigal son's father was not an enabler; he allowed his son to be responsible for his own actions. Being a good father, he was certainly praying for his son, watching for his return, and waiting to receive him with open arms; but he did not send care packages to his son while he was in the hog pen. It is good to know that Jesus is Lord even over the hog pen.

There is a biblical principle that deals with enabling behavior. Paul writes: "Do not be deceived; God cannot be mocked. A man reaps what he sows" (Galatians 6:7). "Praying that God will keep the person from getting into trouble is not helpful. Pray, instead, that God will bring as much trouble into the person's life as it will take to convince him that his life is failing and he is needy" (VanVonderen, 158). As well-intentioned helpers, people may hinder God by their enabling behaviors. Behind their Sunday smiles, many Christians come to church with a heavy heart for a friend or loved one enslaved by a stronghold. Their enabling behaviors may be hindering rather than helping that person's recovery.

As you read this chapter on the various aspects of behavior that contribute to our addictive society, did you see a need for an adjustment or alteration? If so, do not expect change to occur in one day. Begin the process—do what is right and leave the consequences to God.

4

$\mathcal{W}$orking Through the Maze

Having discussed why we are an addictive society, we now turn our attention to the maze that affects our families, churches, schools, and nation. We can conclude we are an addictive society simply because of the massive drug and alcohol problems, sexual immorality, greed, violence, promiscuity, dysfunctional families, and numerous other social ills.

On a coast-to-coast flight, my wife and I could not believe what we saw. The movie that evening had bedroom activities between a man and woman that did not leave room for the imagination. We immediately raised our objections to a flight attendant. She told us that this major airline selected movies that would be popular to the majority of their travelers.

Trying to appease us or perhaps point out our intolerable stance, the flight attendant ask another passenger who had a 10-year-old daughter with her if the movie was inappropriate for them. Unfortunately, the mother did not object to the movie. Thirty thousand feet in the air with no place to go, we were forced to sit through scenes that were embarrassing and humiliating to us. Twenty or thirty years ago, this would not have been accepted.

The question may be asked, "How can you say we are an addictive society when addiction applies to an individual?" The addictive individual in the family affects the entire family, his or her workplace, church, and all walks of life. The reaction to this individual is typically that of negligence or dysfunctional help. Another way to say it is unhelped helpers. This is often caused by distorted thinking. An addictive society develops its own mind-set, frame of reference, and behavioral patterns.

Individuals become slaves to various cravings, but so do groups of people, including nations. The late Richard Halverson, the former Senate chaplain, in his devotional letter for November 7, 1990, recalls a quote from a book entitled *The Decline and Fall of the Athenian Republic* written by Alexander Fraser Tytler who lived at the end of the 18th century and the early part of the 19th (1748-1813).

A democracy cannot exist as a permanent form of government. It can only exist until the voters discover that they can vote themselves money from the Public Treasury. From that moment on the majority always votes for the candidates promising the most benefits from the Public Treasury with a result that a democracy always collapses over loose fiscal policy always followed by dictatorship. The average age of the world's greatest civilizations has been 200 years. These nations have progressed through the following sequence:

From bondage to spiritual faith;
from spiritual faith to great courage;
from courage to liberty;
from liberty to abundance;
from abundance to selfishness;
from selfishness to complacency;
from complacency to apathy;
from apathy to dependency;
from dependency back into bondage.

Tytler shows how a nation can become an addictive society. It is a process that is a downward spiral. Many programs and ministries fail because they overlook the family and social systems of the individual and only address the individual's need. For example, the more effective drug prevention programs establish a broader view of strategies as it relates to the individual.

> Social competencies programs, like purely informational programs, suffer from a significant conceptual flaw, however. They reinforce a view of problems as properties of individuals rather than social systems. . . . Because these problems are linked to the environment of institutions, norms, and community life, it is in the broader context that such problems must be understood (Resnik, 19-20).

We will discuss this further in Chapter 7.

An addictive society is a systems problem clouded by distorted thinking, more commonly known as delusion. The word "maze" helps us describe the term delusion because it is intricately (involving parts or elements) confusing and complicated. Delusion blinds us to the truth. Delusion does not happen accidentally; it occurs and builds lie upon lie when the truth is suppressed. Romans 1:18-32 shows the progression of evil, how it blinds people, and where it starts—those "who suppress the truth by their wickedness" (v18). Let's take a look at how delusion works.

Denial and Delusion

Bob's phone rang at the office one cold, February day, and the caller was the high school principal, Mr. Chambers. Mr. Chambers had some bad news for Bob and his wife, Carolyn. During the lunch hour, their son, Tom, had been caught smoking pot with two other members of the football team. This was particularly tough for Bob and Carolyn since they were strongly committed Christians and had raised Tom according to these values. Also, this was the second time he had been caught at school, and his lifestyle and friends had changed to reflect his chemical use.

Over a period of two to three years, Bob and Carolyn had noticed their son's increasing indifference and unconcern toward their family life. It seemed as though he lived in a world of his own surrounded by walls. After Mr. Chambers' call, Bob took the suggestion of a Christian counselor. He decided to make Tom responsible for his actions. Bob insisted the principal call the police and have Tom arrested. Tom was sent to the juvenile detention center where Bob met his 16-year-old son. Denying he had a problem with chemicals, Tom was irate and accused his father of being a noncaring, worthless parent.

Bob and Carolyn (although she had second thoughts) felt there was no other choice but to send Tom to a treatment program thereby hoping to help him with his dependency. A few months later, Tom's parents were surprised when he thanked them for having him arrested and forced into treatment. He told them he was thankful because at the time of his arrest, he was blind to what was actually happening in his life.

Aspects of Delusion

Denial and delusion are chief characteristics seen in those who are struggling with dependencies. When denial continues over a period of time, it results in delusion. J. Keith Miller in his work on deadly addictions says:

> The two characteristics of the Sin-disease . . . "denial" and "delusion," are almost universal. Denial by definition means not being able to see the ever-widening split between what one says and what one is. . . . Delusion is seeing things that are true and acting as if they are not true. Delusion recreates reality around a person to make it less threatening to his or her self-centered (Sin) position (95).

Delusion is sincere. A wife said to her neglectful husband, "Don't you see what your gambling is doing to the children and to me?" He replied, "It's no big deal. You're the problem, not me." Even though the family was struggling to survive because of his addiction, he sincerely believed his gambling was not affecting them and blamed his wife. Another example of delusion is a young lady, weighing only 85 pounds, staring at herself in the mirror and seeing herself as being fat.

A person in delusion is a person who is misled. "A deluded heart misleads him; he cannot save himself, or say, 'Is not this thing in my right hand a lie?' " (Isaiah 44:20). The Apostle Paul writes in 2 Corinthians 4:4, "The god of this age has blinded the minds of unbelievers, so that they cannot see the light of the gospel of the glory of Christ." They have no sense of reality of the truth because their thinking is distorted. "He will believe his statements to himself such as, 'A little drink never hurt anyone.' 'I've been working hard, I've earned it.' 'Most women are asking to be raped.' 'I can take it or leave it.' 'I'm not really as heavy as people say I am.' 'If you had to live with my wife, you'd drink, too' " (Holwerda and Egner, 7-8).

Delusion is extremely strong because it is very difficult for people to see themselves as they really are. In his work on chemical dependency Jeffrey VanVonderen states:

> Quite some time ago I heard a statistic that has remained with me and has been a great source of comfort to many families with whom I have worked. The statistic states that an average of fifty-four confrontations of his chemical problem are necessary for a dependent person to realize he has a chemical problem. You would think this would be depressing to those who are trying to help a chemically dependent person, but actually it has the potential of being very freeing and encouraging. The statistic means that there is hope, that people eventually realize their need for help. It means that one person does not carry the entire burden of helping someone realize his problem. It means that each individual step or effort is not wasted, even if it appears as such at the time (97).

There is an old adage which is common among many people who have worked with dependent people: "A person must hit bottom before he can get help"; however, a helper can chip away at the denial system and raise the bottom.

The Johari Window

This concept is an effective way to illustrate delusion. The four window panes represent a person's total self. Window pane 1 is *open*. The person and others recognize what is happening in this window. The open information includes things like the weather, sports, vocation, and other interests. Window pane 2 is *secret*. In this window, people have secrets known only to themselves. As a trust relationship is established, they may choose to reveal their secrets to others. Window pane 4 is the *subconscious* part and is not visible to self or others. Window pane 3 is the *blind* area. These are the things that

The Johari Window	
1: OPEN Known to me and openly shared with others.	**2: SECRET** What I know and choose to hide from others.
3: BLIND What others know about me, but I can't see for myself.	**4: SUBCONSCIOUS** The part of me that is hidden to all.

Figure 4-1

are seen by others but not recognized by the individual himself. The person with a stronghold lives mostly in window pane 3. Since such people cannot see the reality of their lives, they will need caring friends who will carefully provide feedback and pray for the Holy Spirit to open their eyes to the truth. In his work on prayer, Charles Stanley states:

Satan pumps us full of lies which secure these strongholds. They may sound like this, "There's really nothing wrong with this music—I don't listen to the words anyway." Or, "I just drink a little when I get nervous." And haven't we all said, "The police won't pull me over for going 60 mph, so it's OK"?

Our responsibility as Christians is to tear down these strongholds through Spirit-filled prayers. How? There is only one weapon—the sword of the Spirit. We must fight these lies with God's Word. We must fight specific lies with specific truths (118).

The Role of Defenses

Defenses play a major role in the lives of those who are in bondage to an addiction. These are behaviors people use to cover up feelings from themselves and others. After a period of time, the deluded individuals begin to believe their own excuses. Defenses are like a fortress surrounding and preventing the conquering of the stronghold, and they keep the victims from seeing the truth of their bondage.

Rationalization is a common defense used among those with a dependency. They give reasons as to why "it's not my fault because" or "everybody is doing it." Blaming is a defense used by our first parents. When the Lord God confronted Adam, he said, "The woman you put here with me—she gave me some fruit from the tree, and I ate it" (Genesis 3:12). When the Lord God confronted Eve, she blamed the serpent (v13).

David after having Uriah murdered to cover up for his sin with Bathsheba, minimized the death of Uriah. Joab sent an account of the battle by a messenger to David stating that some men were killed along with Uriah. When David received the message he replied, "Don't let this upset you; the sword devours one as well as another" (2 Samuel 11:25). By minimizing, David tried to lessen the impact of Uriah's death for which he was responsible.

Denial is a defense that prevents many people from seeing the truth. The most common form is our denial that we need God. A major hurdle for all sinners is to recognize the need for Jesus Christ as Savior and Lord. The Church must be on guard to this sin of denial. As the body of Christ, we need each other; and when we refuse this principle, God is not pleased.

The Pharisees were known for their defense of superiority. They were arrogant and self-righteous. Jesus describes their defense in Luke 18:9: "To some who were confident of their own righteousness and looked down on everybody else." Some people show their defense of superiority when they say, "I don't need to go to church," or "I can hold my liquor." "For the most part defenses, including attitudinal postures, are unintentional and automatic shields against a real or imagined threat to our self-esteem" (Johnson, 135). Sin goes undetected when a person is infatuated with himself. This type of superiority is recorded in Psalm 36:2: "For in his own eyes he flatters himself too much to detect or hate his sin."

The Role of Feelings

David, the director of a Christian home for young men, was walking through the dormitory one morning after chapel when he noticed one of the students weeping openly. Concerned, David asked if he could assist him. Paul replied, "No, sir! I have just come to the realization that God loves me, and it is awesome!" Paul had been in the program for two months. His feelings, not unlike others with dependencies, had been suppressed, and for the first time in many years he could experience feelings again. People with life-controlling problems learn to lie about their feelings, and their emotions become numb over a period of time. Vernon Johnson describes the role of feelings:

> While change is the ultimate goal, our immediate purpose is to see more accurately what needs change. This requires seeing ourselves—*discovering ourself*—and at a feeling level.
>
> In examining our purpose one of the things that stands out is our emphasis on feelings. We stress feelings for several reasons. First of all, our behavior in the past has been so opposed to our value system that considerable feelings of remorse and self-loathing have been

built up. It appears that we have accumulated a pool of negative feelings and walled them off with a variety of masks or *defenses that prevent this discovery* (132).

Concerning the role of feelings, Paul writes in Ephesians 4:19: "Who being past feeling have given themselves over unto lasciviousness, to work all uncleanness with greediness" (KJV). In this passage he is encouraging the church at Ephesus not to live in delusion. They were warned not to be caught up in futile thinking, darkened understanding, and hardness of heart. These characteristics of delusion led to the numbness of feelings and the acting out of all kinds of impurities and moral uncleanness. In this passage Paul also describes the sin-disease as progressive. They had a "continual lust for more" (v19). Deceitful desires are associated with the old self (*see* 4:22).

The Bible provides several examples of people who express their feelings. When Jesus approached Jerusalem during the triumphal entry and saw the city, "he wept over it" (Luke 19:41). Jesus also showed his feelings along with Mary and Martha at the death of Lazarus (*see* John 11:17-44). After Peter disowned Jesus for the third time, "he went outside and wept bitterly" (Matthew 26:75). In the Book of Psalms, there are a number of passages in which David expresses both positive and negative feelings (*see* Psalm 32; 38; 51; 55; 56; 71; 73; 139; 143; 147). When David brought the ark of God into Jerusalem, he expressed euphoric feelings by dancing before the Lord with all his might (*see* 2 Samuel 6:14). David experienced the opposite feelings when he received the news that his conspiring son Absalom was dead. The author of 2 Samuel 18:33 writes, "The king was shaken. He went up to the room over the gateway and wept. As he went, he said: 'O my son Absalom! My son, my son Absalom! If only I had died instead of you—O Absalom, my son, my son!'" David did not suppress his extreme feelings of sorrow. Although David's sin with Bathsheba caused him much pain, he effectively dealt with his feelings by expressing and taking ownership of them through a repentant heart.

Unlike the belief system of many secularists who assert that feelings are neither good nor bad, the Bible teaches otherwise. There are sinful and nonsinful feelings. Sinful feelings include jealousy, greed, and lust; whereas, grief and sorrow can be described as non-sinful feelings. Both sinful and nonsinful feelings are real. To deny them leads to their burial and a possible explosion. Keith Miller states:

> Our feelings constitute a wonderful "warning system" that tells us when we need to focus on a certain danger area in our lives or something that needs our love and attention. These feelings can activate energy and guidance to keep us safe, to heal our hurts, and to help us follow our highest ideals. But when we are in denial we bury these feelings, push them into our unconscious like pushing giant beach balls under water. . . . And when a feeling does get loose it comes up with exaggerated force "at an angle" and may hurt someone, like a beach ball that has been pushed far under water and finally pops to the surface (101).

Not only did Jesus express his feelings while on earth, but He is also concerned about our emotions. The letter written to the Hebrews emphasizes Christ's exalted position at the right hand of the Father as our high priest; however, even with his record of perfection, He still identifies with our feelings. "For we have not an high priest which cannot be touched with the feeling of our infirmities; but was in all points tempted like as *we are, yet* without sin" (Hebrews 4:15 KJV). Since He understands and sympathizes with our feelings, the writer of Hebrews encourages us to "approach the throne of grace with confidence, so that we may receive mercy and find grace to help us in our time of need" (4:16).

Without question, Jesus understands the damage that can be done when feelings are stuffed. We are urged by him to approach "the kingdom of God like a little child" (Mark 10:15). Little children are quick to trust in Jesus, and they are also willing to share their feelings.

Paul writes: "Brothers, stop thinking like children. In regard to evil be infants, but in your thinking be adults" (1 Corinthians 14:20). "One does not expect a small child to understand spiritual things... On the other hand, children do not develop deep-seated malice or habitual faultfinding. They are quick to forgive and for-get" (S. Horton, 228-229). Paul recognizes the negative elements of suppressed feelings. He urges the church at Corinth to have under-standing as adults but to be like children in regard to their emo-tions: don't stuff them. He also warns the church at Ephesus against the buildup of anger. He does not discourage anger; however, he does say in Ephesians 4:26-27, "Do not let the sun go down while you are still angry, and do not give the devil a foothold."

It is common for persons in delusion to build a wall of defenses around themselves which helps them suppress and harden their feelings. There are many examples of delusion throughout the Bible. When Moses led the children of Israel out of bondage, they became blind to what God had done for them. God sent Isaiah to people who could hear but not understand and could see but not perceive.

Jesus recognized the delusion while He was on this earth. In Matthew 13:13, He describes delusion as: "Though seeing, they do not see; though hearing, they do not hear or understand." Jesus rec-ognized a degree of delusion among His own disciples. He asked them some thought-provoking questions recorded in Mark 8:18, "Do you have eyes but fail to see, and ears but fail to hear?"

All of us have the potential of having a life-controlling problem. Through the means of permissiveness that has slowly and persis-tently infiltrated our society and the Church, delusion has increased. Using a human point of view versus the biblical point of view, standards and sin are being redefined in some circles. Refusing to acknowledge sin results in compounding sin. When ignored or unconfessed, sins build on each other causing delusion which can affect individuals (including the innocent), families, and even nations. Isaiah warns (30:1), " 'Woe to the obstinate children,' declares the LORD, 'to those who carry out plans that are not mine, forming an alliance, but not by my Spirit, heaping sin upon sin.' "

The Bible is being attacked by those within and without the Church. To survive as a nation, we must ultimately realize there is no way to measure truth apart from the Bible. Our massive prob-lems of drugs, alcohol, greediness, incest, and so forth are fed by various delusions. The writer to the Hebrews says: "For the word of God is living and active. . . . it judges the thoughts and attitudes of the heart. Nothing in all creation is hidden from God's sight. Everything is uncovered and laid bare before the eyes of him to whom we must give account" (4:12-13).

5

$\mathcal{H}$ow the Spiritual Battle Is Waged and Won

The Apostle Paul made an important response to the mind-set of the Corinthians, "Everything is permissible for me." He went on to say, "but I will not be mastered by anything" (1 Corinthians 6:12). This statement was not made as a "sound bite" or from a cliché he read in a church bulletin. He made this statement with much substance. He understood fully how to do battle with Satan and be an overcomer.

First, he understood spiritual warfare. He said, "For though we live in the world, we do not wage war as the world does. The weapons we fight with are not the weapons of the world. On the contrary, they have divine power to demolish strongholds. We demolish arguments and every pretension that sets itself up against the knowledge of God, and we take captive every thought to make it obedient to Christ" (2 Corinthians 10:3-5).

Paul refused to manipulate people intellectually although he was very intelligent. He did not use personal charm through his speech, nor did he use empty philosophical or psychological jargon to impress people with his knowledge of human behavior.

Instead, he focused on God to overpower the strongholds that were mastering the people.

Paul deals with one of the great areas of defeat of many Christians in this passage when he says, "We demolish arguments and every pretension that sets itself up against the knowledge of God." The battle in today's society is in the mind. To wage war against Satan, we must first demolish, cast down those imaginations, speculations, or even reasonings and logics that come against the truth of God's Word.

What do we do with those imaginations that trouble the Christians' minds? We bring our thought life, our framework of thought, into obedience to Christ. A daily time of prayer and Bible reading cultivates the soil of the mind and keeps us in active fellowship with Christ. John writes, "And our fellowship is with the Father and with his Son, Jesus Christ" (1 John 1:3).

> The basis of our immaturity is self-centeredness that keeps us from fellowship with God, ourselves, our brother, nature, and life itself. Every immature person is tied in on himself and cannot be outgoing, friendly, and loving—cannot have fellowship. So the first thing in the Christian purpose is to produce fellowship. . . . The person who has no fellowship with God is an immature person (Jones, 25).

Second, Paul understood the character of Satan which was built on lies; therefore, his plan of attack or method of schemes would be devices and trickery. Paul said, "For we are not unaware of his schemes" (2 Corinthians 2:11). It is important that we understand the schemes the enemy is using to get us out-of-focus on Christ. He has three favorite tools that we all face.

Out-of-Focus

A few years ago, my wife and I went on a "whale watch" in Hawaii. Concerned about seasickness, we asked the captain the best thing to do to prevent it while sailing the ocean. He directed us to focus our eyes on an object and not on the waves. When traveling in the beautiful mountains of Tennessee with our guests, I have noticed it is usually the backseat passenger who feels sick and not the driver. Why? Because the driver is focused.

It is the same principal in serving Christ. When we get out-of-focus by turning our sole attention to the waves of life, we will get sick. There are two prescriptions that will help us stay spiritually and emotionally well. First, "Let us fix our eyes on Jesus" (Hebrews 12:2). Next, look up, not down. In Psalm 8, David proclaims the name of the Lord and says, "You made him a little lower than the heavenly beings and crowned him with glory and honor" (v5). In verses 6-8, he tells how flocks and herds, beast of the field, and so forth, are under man. There is a significant point in this passage we need to see. We were made a little lower that the heavenly beings, not a little higher than the animal kingdom.

> It could have been written the other way around. If man really is a mediating being, as the Psalm maintains, it would have been equally accurate to have described him as slightly higher than the beasts rather than as slightly lower than the angels. Although men and women have been given a position midway between the angels and the beasts, it is nevertheless humanity's special privilege and duty to look upward to the angels (and beyond the angels to God, in whose image woman and man have been made) rather than downward to the beasts (Boice, 70-71).

We have been made in the image of God; therefore, we are to look up, not down. It is not surprising that the proponents of evolution work diligently to trace man's origin to the animal kingdom. In their view, if there is no God, what other choice is available?

When we get out-of-focus, our attention will likely be directed to an idol. The second commandment says:

> You shall not make for yourself an idol in the form of anything in heaven above or on the earth beneath or in the waters below. You shall not bow down to them or worship them; for I, the LORD your God, am a jealous God, punishing the children for the sin of the fathers to the third and fourth generation of those who hate me,

but showing love to a thousand generations of those who love me
and keep my commandments (Exodus 20:4-6).

Built on the first commandment, this commandment tells us that
man is going to worship something and that God is a jealous God (2
Corinthians 11:2). We are forbidden to worship or use created
things or even creation itself as an approach to God. Idols become
God-substitutes and can include the environment (trees, flowers,
ocean, land, etc.), church buildings, drugs, alcohol, money, statues,
monuments, tradition, and the list goes on. These idols are often
handed down to the next generation. (This will be discussed in
more detail in Chapter 7.)

An idol becomes a focal point in our lives even though it has no
helping power or substance. The power of influence is not in the
idol but the one behind the idol—our enemy Satan. He uses idols
to get us out-of-focus. Paul says, "Put to death, therefore, whatever
belongs to your earthly nature: sexual immorality, impurity, lust, evil
desires and greed, which is idolatry" (Colossians 3:5). In Ephesians
5:5, Paul says an "immoral, impure or greedy person . . . is an idol-
ater." Jealousy is also an idol (Ezekiel 8:5).

Paul says, "We know that an idol is nothing at all in the world and
that there is no God but one" (1 Corinthians 8:4). He also notes
from where the influence of an idol comes: "Do I mean then that a
sacrifice offered to an idol is anything, or that an idol is anything?
No, but the sacrifices of pagans are offered to demons, not to God,
and I do not want you to be participants with demons" (1
Corinthians 10:19-20). Paul goes on to say that this arouses "the
Lord's jealousy. Are we stronger than he" (1 Corinthians 10:22)?
God is jealous on our behalf because He knows our loyalty to Him
is important for our well-being.

As human beings, we are frail and weak, and idols only add baggage to our lives. Jeremiah says, "they must be carried because they
cannot walk" (10:5). What about the conversation, kindness, or
friendship of an idol? "They have mouths, but cannot speak . . .
they have hands, but cannot feel" (Psalm 115:5,7). What about the
outcome or benefit from trusting an idol? "Those who make them
will be like them, and so will all who trust in them" (Psalm 115:8).

David said, "My eyes are ever on the LORD, for only he will release my feet from the snare" (Psalm 25:15).

Three Tools of Satan

There are three active tools every person needs to be aware of that Satan is using to reinforce an addictive society. The first is delusion. We have already talked about this in Chapter 4, but remember it is a false belief system or seeing things that are true and acting as though they are not true. Isaiah 44:20 presents a vivid picture of delusion as the prophet addresses those who are serving idols: "He feeds on ashes, a deluded heart misleads him; he cannot save himself, or say, 'Is not this thing in my right hand a lie?' " It is possible to have an idol in our right hand and not see it. For example, a person controlled by a substance, behavior, or relationship is often blind to the destruction he is causing his family and himself.

Another favorite tool of Satan is isolation. When faced with a struggle, feelings of failure, or when a destructive stronghold develops in our lives, we often move into isolation by building a wall around ourselves. We sometimes go to church with our "Sunday smiles" and sit in our own "private phone booth." There are probably others on the same pew who are also in isolation. I have heard this statement many times: "I was dying on the inside, but it seemed that no one cared." I believe this statement is often incorrect; it just seems that way because isolation often separates us in an addictive society when we need each other so much. "As the problem intensifies, their delusional system allows them to justify their isolation. Since they've learned to lie to themselves, lying to others is easy. Gradually they hold onto their idol with both hands, turning their back on the only One who offers them hope for deliverance" (Perkins, 39). It is not wise to isolate ourselves from those who care for us. "A man who isolates himself seeks his own desire; He rages against all wise judgment" (Proverbs 18:1 NKJV).

The third tool is secrecy, or another way to describe it is hiding. Life-controlling problems grow in the soil of secrecy. Sweeping sin under the rug may hide it for a while, but it will eventually surface.

When Adam and Eve sinned, "they hid from the LORD God among the trees of the garden" (Genesis 3:8). Hiding the use of an addictive substance, the practice of a destructive behavior, or the development of an unhealthy relationship often develops into worship of that substance, behavior, or person. Isaiah describes this: "for we have made a lie our refuge and falsehood (or false gods) our hiding place" (28:15).

Everyone will have a hiding place. I hear people say, "He hides himself in his work, education, drugs, alcohol, etc." God recognizes this need we have for a hiding place. Paul says, "For you died, and your life is now hidden with Christ in God" (Colossians 3:3).

Several years ago there was a popular book, *The Hiding Place*, which was about the faith and courage of Corrie ten Boom. During World War II, her family hid Jews from the Nazis in their home in Haarlem, Holland. This house, which had a clock shop on the first floor, was a refuge for Jews. The Nazi police would frequent the shop; therefore, there were certain symbols in the window which would indicate it was safe for Jews to enter the house.

My wife and I have visited the famous refuge in Haarlem on two occasions. We were told by those who knew Corrie ten Boom and her sister, Betsie, that Betsie's prayer was not focused on the safety of her family or the Jews. Her prayers were focused on the saving of the Nazis. Betsie ten Boom really knew who her "hiding place" was. It was more than a building. Her mind was set "on things above, not on earthly things" (Colossians 3:2).

Delusion, isolation, and secrecy all work together in the life of a person who is developing a life-controlling problem (a substance, behavior, or relationship that is mastering a person's life). When a person suppresses the truth, withdraws himself from those who care, and hides his actions, the journey has started to a problem that will end up mastering the person if corrective action is not taken.

God's Three Primary Resources

As in past decades, we have God's resources to defeat Satan's lies and schemes of delusion, isolation, and secrecy. First, we have the

Word of God. "For the word of God is living and active. Sharper than any double-edged sword, it penetrates even to dividing soul and spirit, joints and marrow; it judges the thoughts and attitudes of the heart. Nothing in all creation is hidden from God's sight. Everything is uncovered and laid bare before the eyes of him to whom we must give account" (Hebrews 4:12-13). What about the Word of God in this addictive society in which we live? Psalm 119: 89-90 declares, "Your word, O LORD, is eternal; it stands firm in the heavens. Your faithfulness continues through all generations." "Our responsibility is to tear down . . . strongholds through Spirit-filled prayers. How? There is only one weapon–the sword of the Spirit. We must fight these lies with God's Word. We must fight specific lies with specific truths" (Stanley, 118).

Second, we have the Spirit of God. "But when he, the Spirit of truth, comes, he will guide you into all truth" (John 16:13). Through the Holy Spirit, believers "put to death the misdeeds of the body" (Romans 8:13). Believers are "led by the Spirit of God" (Romans 8:14). Whether the Holy Spirit leads by inward urgings or by circumstances, His direction is always in God's will, in agreement with the Scripture, and in opposition to the sinful nature. We have the promise of the Holy Spirit to guide us through the maze of deception in this addictive society. Being our counselor, the Holy Spirit will make Jesus known to us in a personal way.

Third, we have the people of God. We have each other. The New Testament presents the Church as the people of God on numerous occasions with the words "one another" (love one another, bear with one another, comfort one another, forgive one another, etc.). Hebrews 3:13 points to the importance of the "one another" relationship: "But encourage one another daily, as long as it is called Today, so that none of you may be hardened by sin's deceitfulness." The picture of this verse can be seen as a long distance race, and the runner is weary and perhaps ready to give up. The encourager comes alongside him to offer support, encouraging the runner not to give up. This verse also shows the importance of the personal care for each other—"encourage one another . . . so that none of you . . . " The "one another" care is to be regular—"daily." It is more than *friend day* once a year. The word *Today* implies urgency. Now is the time.

Why are "one another" relationships important? "So that none of you may be hardened [a process] by sin's deceitfulness [the delusion of sin]." We need an active relationship with Jesus Christ and one another in this addictive society. Building relationships with one another can be hard work, but it is essential whether it is in a Sunday school class, home group, office staff, cell group, or support group. You need the people of God. The people of God need you.

The people of God are "God's fellow workers" (1 Corinthians 3:9). The death of Lazarus as recorded in John 11 is an example of Jesus and the people of God. Mary and her sister, Martha, sent word to Jesus that Lazarus, their brother and a friend of Jesus, was very sick. Jesus loved Mary, Martha, and Lazarus but stayed two more days before leaving for their home.

When Jesus arrived, he "found that Lazarus had already been in the tomb for four days" (v17). There were already many Jews there to comfort Martha and Mary in the loss of their brother. It is noteworthy that Lazarus means "God is his help." In this passage are four principles of help that are involved in being in partnership with Christ.

There Is Help for the Ifs in Life

" 'Lord,' Martha said to Jesus, 'If you had been here, my brother would not have died' " (v21). Martha was saying, "You're too late Jesus; my brother is already dead. Thanks for coming to show your concern." The words, "if you had" or "if I had only," speak of the past. There are relationships and circumstances in the past you cannot change. This was a situation Martha could not change—her brother was dead and had been dead for four days.

There have been times in life when we felt Jesus was tardy or not there at the time when we needed help. Even at a low time in Martha's life when all hope was gone, Jesus had a plan to help her with the past. The lesson here—let us place in the trust of Jesus the "ifs" of the past in our lives.

In the book, *The Hiding Place*, Corrie ten Boom tells of a night when German and English planes were dogfighting above them in the skies over Holland. After hearing her sister Betsie stirring in the kitchen, Corrie raced down. For an hour, they sipped tea together until the sky was silent.

Corrie returned to her bed in a darkened room. She ran her hand over the pillow and felt a piece of metal. There was a ten-inch piece of metal that had fallen onto her bed. She rushed to tell Betsie, " 'Betsie, if I hadn't heard you in the kitchen—' But Betsie put a finger on my mouth. 'Don't say it, Corrie! There are no "ifs" in God's world. And no places that are safer than other places. The center of His will is our only safety—O Corrie, let us pray that we may always know it!' " (ten Boom, 67).

There Is Help for the Hurts in Life

"When Mary reached the place where Jesus was and saw him, she fell at his feet and said, 'Lord, if you had been here, my brother would not have died.' When Jesus saw her weeping, and the Jews who had come along with her also weeping, he was deeply moved in spirit and troubled" (vv32-33). Mary took her hurts to Jesus— "she fell at his feet." Being deeply touched by their sorrow, "Jesus wept" (v35). The old hymn says it well, "What a friend we have in Jesus, all our sins and grief to bear. What a privilege to carry everything to God in prayer."

There Is Help to Help Yourself

When Jesus came to the tomb, he ask for assistance in removing the stone at the entrance of the cave. After the stone was removed, Jesus prayed to the Father then "called in a loud voice, 'Lazarus, come out!' The dead man came out, his hands and feet wrapped with strips of linen" (vv43-44). Notice, Jesus asked him to do all he could do, and Lazarus did all he could do to help himself. Jesus will not do what we can do for ourselves. What we cannot do for ourselves, He is there to help.

Hand–in–Hand Help

Throughout this passage, we see Jesus and the people of God working together. The people of God called for help, shared sorrow, removed the stone, and Lazarus did his part. However, the climactic display of hand-in-hand help was when Jesus said to the people of God, "Take off the grave clothes and let him go" (v44). Jesus raised Lazarus from the dead, so was he not capable of removing the grave clothing? Certainly He was! However, He chose to have a partnership by involving the people of God in removing the grave clothes.

God involves each of us in this spiritual battle we face living in an "addictive society." To deal with the delusion, isolation, and secrecy, we need the Word of God, the Spirit of God, and each other.

6

Common Hurdles and Helps

Creating the right kind of environment for a person to receive help is essential for individuals, families, and churches. This addictive society and the deception it perpetrates are hurdles that well-meaning parents, teachers, ministers, and church workers all face. In this chapter we will discuss various helping skills to overcome hurdles.

In the previous chapters we have talked about the maze of deception and three main contributing factors: delusion, isolation, and secrecy. The helper can easily become a part of the problem instead of a part of the solution. Helping a friend or family member who is controlled by a mastering problem will be a spiritual battle. Although prayer and concern are essential, it is important to use common sense in dealing with a person who is being influenced by this addictive society.

Whether it is a son on drugs, a daughter with an eating disorder, or a husband hooked on pornography, the helper must remember that recovery is a process. Paul said, "I planted the seed, Apollos watered it, but God made it grow" (1 Corinthians 3:6). Do all you can and trust God to bring appropriate people into the person's life. You may be the planter of help and see no change in the person's life. Do not give up. Pray and ask God to bring an Apollos helper to water your work. Planting and watering creates the environment for God to work in your friend's or loved one's life.

Communicating With People in Delusion

People who are enslaved to a stronghold are difficult to communicate with because denial has led them to blindness of their condition. Jim Holwerda and David Egner in their work on addiction state:

> The fantasy world of an addict is more important to him than the real world. As he lets his thoughts go, he becomes convinced that the scenario he constructs to support his addiction is true. When shoplifters are caught, for example, they are often startled. The reality of the truth that they were stealing had been distorted. They had not realistically considered that they might face arrest or jail or embarrassment—the real consequences of their behavior. . . .
>
> Along with distortion is a breakdown in logical thinking. The addicted person, for example, refuses to link alcohol abuse with impaired driving. Or sexual sin with a threat to his marriage. Or compulsive spending with bankruptcy.
>
> The Lord was crystal-clear in the Scriptures in setting forth the principle of sowing and reaping. But the addicted person won't accept it because he isn't thinking straight. He may often say when caught, "I can't believe it was me doing this. . . ."
>
> The addicted person actually begins to believe the lies he tells himself to justify his habit (7).

Communication with those who have life-controlling problems is extremely important because with each communication there is a chipping away of the person's denial system. Communication is more effective when it lessens the defensive mechanisms of the person with a stronghold yet communicates the truth in a caring way.

Careful Confrontation

After concluding his sermon on Wednesday evening, Max was greeted by Martha. With tears in her eyes, she requested an appointment for her and her husband, Ed, to discuss their son, Gary. He was home from college for the summer, and his behavior was causing these Christian parents much pain.

On the following day, Ed and Martha revealed to Max that Gary's grades had plunged near the failing level. The university was about to remove his athletic scholarship for many rule infractions, and the clincher was when he came home intoxicated last Friday evening. Gary was considered a leader in his church youth group and had been a top-notch student in high school. He was respected by his peers and coaches, so these events in Gary's life over the past year concerned his parents.

An appointment was made for Gary to talk with Max. Although Gary honored the appointment, he did so with a great deal of indifference toward Max. Over a period of nine sessions, Max and Gary met together with Max care-fronting Gary concerning the downward spiral of his life which appeared to be because of the development of an addiction. Max used the care-fronting principles by David Augsburger which include focusing feedback on: the action, not the actor, observations, not conclusions; descriptions, not judgments; ideas, information, and alternatives, not advice and answers; what and how, not why (Augsburger, 54-56).

Feedback on action, not the actor. Max complimented Gary as a person but focused his discussion on his behavior. He did this to give Gary the freedom to change without feeling personal rejection. Max was careful not to criticize Gary as a person; instead, he focused on his coming home intoxicated, poor grades, and discipline infractions which were threatening his football scholarship. When Gary tried to attack Max with a war of words, Max always brought the discussion back to the facts of Gary's behavior. It is important to focus on the person's behavior versus the person as an individual. Emphasis should be placed on what he does rather than on attacking him personally.

Feedback on observations, not conclusions. Max focused on statements of facts instead of what he thought or imagined. Max noticed Gary would not look at him, was not giving him his full attention, and seemed anxious for the discussion to conclude. Observing these actions, Max brought them to Gary's attention. A conclusion that Gary was a drunk without respect for his parents was never suggested.

Focusing on what the helper has actually seen or heard from the other person can serve as a guard against interpretation of behavior. When a helper interprets the behavior of the one seeking help, the helper may be seen as jumping to conclusions.

Feedback on descriptions, not judgments. Max never judged Gary's behavior as being good or bad. Communication lines remained open with 20-year-old Gary because Max never placed a value judgment on his behavior. Communications were directed toward the descriptions of Gary's behavior in neutral language. Max described in detail each of the behaviors Gary confessed over a period of nine weeks thereby helping him see the clear facts of the downward spiral of his life. By giving descriptions, the helper is more likely to be seen in a neutral role as reporting on what has been seen rather than on the behavior as right or wrong.

Feedback on ideas, information, and alternatives, not on advice and answers. During the last three meetings, Max began to focus with Gary on the various options open to him. Continuing to drink alcohol was an option Gary could select. Max explained the steps of the addiction process, and Gary noted he was in the latter part of stage three. Although he told his parents he had been intoxicated only two times in college, Gary disclosed to Max he was drunk in excess of thirty times during the school year.

Max was careful not to use scare tactics, give pat answers, or even specifically advise Gary what to do. When Gary finally asked Max for help, Max directed him first to the Lord to mend this relationship. Next he provided Gary with positive options from which he could choose. These options included continued meetings with him, a meeting with his parents in Max's presence, attending a college in his hometown, and entering a support group at church.

When the helper is providing ideas, information, and alternatives, the receiver of the help is free to select options. When the helper gives advice and answers, the one seeking help may not accept personal responsibility. It may restrain the freedom of the receiver of help to chart a personal course of action because of dependence on the advice of another person. The seeker may also resent the helper who insists on giving advice and answers.

Feedback on what and how, not on why. Max was careful not to ask Gary why he was intoxicated over thirty times during the school year or why he would disgrace his Christian parents with such deviant behavior. Max knew using the word *why* would only serve to raise Gary's defenses and make it more difficult to penetrate his state of delusion. Open-ended sentences using *what* and *how* were used in Max's communications with him so Gary would not feel his motives or values were being critiqued.

Observable behaviors can be described by words such as *what*, *how*, *when*, and *where*. *Why* may break the communication because it may serve to raise the other person's defenses by questioning his motives. Although his motives may be wrong, his delusion can be penetrated best by observed facts presented in a nonthreatening way through a helper who is depending on the Holy Spirit's guidance.

Care-fronting is a way to help communicate the truth in love thus creating an environment for healing and growth. Paul writes in Ephesians 4:15: "Speaking the truth in love, we will in all things grow up into him who is the Head, that is, Christ." Helpers should avoid trying to convict a person with a life-controlling problem to produce changed behavior. Conviction is a work of the Holy Spirit. In regard to the Holy Spirit, Jesus says in John 16:8: "When he comes, he will convict the world of guilt in regard to sin and righteousness and judgment."

John 8 records the account of the woman caught in the act of adultery. The scribes and Pharisees tried to use the law of Moses to trap Jesus by insisting she be stoned to death. Jesus responded to them by saying "If any one of you is without sin, let him be the first to throw a stone at her" (v7). Her accusers then left one by one. After they left, Jesus care-fronted the lady and said, "Then neither do I condemn you" [caring] . . . "Go now and leave your life of sin" [confronting] (v11).

The person enslaved by a stronghold is already under condemnation. The victim needs freedom in Christ, not further condemnation. John writes in 3:17: "For God did not send his Son into the world to condemn the world, but to save the world through him." David Augsburger in his work on careful confrontation states:

> Truth and love are the two necessary ingredients for any relationship with integrity. Love—because all positive relationships begin with friendship, appreciation, respect. And truth—because no relationship of trust can long grow from dishonesty, deceit, betrayal; it springs up from the solid stuff of integrity.
>
> "Confrontation plus caring brings growth just as judgment plus grace brings salvation," says Howard Clinebell, Jr., a well-known pastoral counselor. . . .
>
> Judgment cuts, even kills. If God dealt with us only in judgment, who could stand? If God reached out to us only in love, it would be a cheap grace without integrity. Mere divine permissiveness. "Anything goes" as far as heaven is concerned. Not so!(20)

Care-fronters and the convicting work of the Holy Spirit go hand in hand in freeing a person from a life-controlling problem.

I-Messages versus You-Messages

You-messages tend to increase conflict by enhancing the other person's defense mechanism. These messages may cause the other person to feel put down, rejected, resistant, or unimportant. Examples of you-messages include: "You just don't care"; "You are a problem"; "Can't you . . . ?"; "You are so . . . " These types of messages hinder communication with addicted persons because they may feel attacked, labeled, or worthless.

I-messages are more effective than you-messages. I-messages tell what a person feels or how the other person's behavior is affecting him or her. This type of message helps to communicate feelings regarding the other person's behavior and the effect of it without strengthening the defenses of the other person.

I-messages deal with facts versus evaluation. They help to communicate honesty and openness. I-messages are less likely to cause harm to the relationship because the self-esteem of the other person is not attacked. An I-message is different from a you-message in that the speaker takes the responsibility for personal feelings. Examples of I-messages include: "I feel very angry because . . . "; "I feel rejected"; "I feel hurt." Paul writes in Colossians 4:6: "Let your conversation be always full of grace, seasoned with salt, so that you may know how to answer everyone." I-messages are tools to be used when the other person has strong feelings or a life-controlling problem. It is important to use nonjudgmental messages when dealing with people who are in delusion.

Active Listening

Active listening is perhaps the most important communication tool in helping people. It demonstrates that the helper is a caring person. It shows that the helper accepts and respects the other person. Empathetic understanding is shown by the helper.

Restating what the other person said conveys that he or she is being heard and that the helper is listening. Being a mirror, reflecting back to the person with a dependency, clarifies distorted thinking. Summarizing pulls together the other person's message and draws it to a concluding point based on what the helper has seen and heard in the conversation.

Active listening is effective in building new relationships. The helper can better understand what the person is saying by being a good listener. This helps to build the trust level and assists the person who is experiencing numb feelings to get in touch with personal emotions. Communication by active listening is a way to build

up persons with a life-controlling problem by showing them they
are accepted. Paul writes in 2 Corinthians 10:8: "For even if I boast
somewhat freely about the authority the Lord gave us for building
you up rather than pulling you down, I will not be ashamed of it."

Active listening is not effective when the person with a stronghold is out of control (intoxicated, severely depressed) since immediate action may be needed. Biblical values and rules should never
be betrayed in favor of active listening.

Effective listening is giving full attention to the person seeking
help. It involves an active reception of the person's message without
being passive. A helper may need to wait during periods of silence
or even tears to get to the real pains the person is experiencing. Eye
contact with appropriate receptive gestures will help the person
know the helper is giving full attention. James writes in 1:19:
"Everyone should be quick to listen, slow to speak and slow to
become angry."

Benefits of Leveling

As Max met with Gary over the nine-week period concerning his
alcohol use while away in college, Gary gradually leveled with him.
At first he would not admit to having a problem; however, Max continued to listen actively to Gary using care-fronting principles. Max
penetrated his delusion by using *I-messages* which did not raise
Gary's defenses. Layer-by-layer and step-by-step, Max carefully led
Gary to the realization that he had a serious problem with alcohol.
Seeing his powerlessness to overcome his problem without the Lord
and caring friends, Gary began to level.

Leveling is the key to breaking out of delusion. The helper should assist
the person with a dependency in leveling with God, self, and others.
Luke provides the account of the tax collector leveling with God:
"But the tax collector stood at a distance. He would not even look
up to heaven, but beat his breast and said, 'God, have mercy on me,
a sinner' " (18:13). Because the tax collector leveled, God granted
this man justification. The opposite of leveling is covering up or
using defenses to protect oneself from the truth. "If we confess our

sins, he is faithful and just and will forgive us our sins and purify us from all unrighteousness" (1 John 1:9).

When a person enslaved with a stronghold shoots straight with the helper, the person is leveling. Vernon Johnson in his work on alcoholism states:

> To respond openly to being confronted is to level. We level when we take the risk of being known by spontaneously reporting our feelings. For example: We level when we let someone know we are hurt—or afraid—or angry.

> Using these feelings as an example of leveling is probably useful for two reasons. Anger bottled up, or fear that is kept hidden seem to lead to more relapses than any other feelings. Also, anger and fear (along with affection) are usually the hardest feelings for us to report. . . .

> If, instead of leveling, we respond without naming a feeling, we are hiding (136).

Intervention

When dependency reaches a point at which people are hurting themselves and do not know they need help, a guided intervention may be necessary. Intervention is an attempt to change an influencing force that is destroying a person's well-being.

The principle of intervention is certainly not new since the Bible records interventions into the destructive behavior of many people. Genesis 3 gives an account of God's first intervention with the first parents of the human race. After Adam and Eve's act of disobedience, they needed a recovery program, and we have been in need of recovery since that time. When they hid themselves from God among the trees, He sought a conversation with them asking, "Where are you?" (Genesis 3:9). God was keenly aware of their fallen condition and obviously knew their whereabouts, but He wanted

a response from them. Through this intervention, God helped
them see their condition, held them responsible for their actions,
and provided a way out of their web of deception.

After David took Uriah's wife, Bathsheba, and then had Uriah
murdered in an effort to cover up their sin, the Lord sent Nathan
to intervene in David's destructive course. Nathan sought a
response by telling him about two men in a certain community: one
was rich and the other was poor (*see* 2 Samuel 12). When a traveler
came to the rich man for a meal, the rich man would not give him
one of his own sheep. Instead, he took the only ewe lamb the poor
man had, one that had grown up with his family, and prepared it for
the traveler. After hearing the story, David responded with anger
toward the rich man, suggesting his death. Nathan then said to
David, "You are the man!" (v7). Nathan discussed the consequences
of David's behavior, and David acknowledged he had sinned against
the Lord. The Lord used Nathan to conduct an intervention on
David to help him see his sinful condition, its long-term consequences, his need for repentance, and how to get back on the track
of recovery.

Showing guided level-by-level interventions, Jesus deals with the
principle of restoration in Matthew 18:15-17. He begins with an *early
intervention*: "If your brother sins against you, go and show him his
fault, just between the two of you" (v15). Early intervention should
be done privately with careful confrontation based on observations
(show him his faults), not with judgment and condemnation. This
should be done soon after the fault has been observed to prevent
delusion. If the brother in the wrong responds favorably, then the
issue is over with and restoration accomplished.

If the brother does not respond to early intervention, he is probably in a state of delusion. The next step, *intermediate intervention,* is
described in verse 16: "But if he will not listen, take one or two others along, so that 'every matter may be established by the testimony
of two or three witnesses.' " There should be descriptive facts presented based on times, places, people affected, and so forth, as they
relate specifically to the problem.

The third level of restoration is *crisis intervention*. "If he refuses to listen to them, tell it to the church; and if he refuses to listen even to the church, treat him as you would a pagan or a tax collector" (v17). At this level the church should already have a plan in place to assist this person if he is repentant and shows a willingness to receive help. If not, he should be made aware of the church's continued love and compassion for him, but the church members will lovingly detach themselves from him until he shows evidence of wanting to change.

This principle of intervention shows three levels with people being added at each phase. All involved are people who are meaningful in his life. To prevent gossip, it is important to inform only those who need to know. The purpose of intervention is to help people, not tear them down.

How does the local church intervene when a person's addictive behavior reaches a crisis stage? After the individual has been approached with early and intermediate intervention without success, who should be involved in the crisis intervention—the entire church body or just a few meaningful people in the person's life? *A crisis intervention should involve only meaningful people.* Involving the entire local church body would probably include enablers, carnal Christians, and those who do not understand addictive behaviors which would hamper restoration.

An effective intervention requires much planning since it is a process. Louis B. and Elizabeth Krupnick in their book, *From Despair to Decision*, present an approach to the process of a guided intervention which is adaptable to the local church (55).

First, there must be a time of assessment to gather information about the person, the family, others who care about the individual, and the person who will lead the intervention process. Certain questions should be asked. Do the concerned persons have the emotional stability to be involved in the process and follow-up? Does the information from the concerned persons indicate the individual is dependent and unable to seek help voluntarily? Is the person who will direct this intervention caring and compassionate?

Will the pastor or a member of the pastoral staff be involved to provide spiritual direction? If the interventionist, pastor, and family
members decide a formal crisis intervention may be helpful, there
should be a meeting to help the family understand intervention
techniques.

The family members need to understand not only the dynamics
of dependency but also how the entire family will be affected. They
should understand codependency (which will be discussed later)
and enabling behaviors as well as the role defenses and feelings play
in the dependent person's life. It is important for the family to
understand that dependencies will normally get worse before they
get better. Since addictive behaviors are progressive, the person is
unlikely to get help on his or her own. With life already out of control, the dependent person probably lives in a state of crisis. The
family members should understand that a directed intervention is
a way for them to begin to take action—at their initiation—with a
controlled crisis.

After the family has been educated, an intervention team should
be selected. Along with the interventionist, the team can include
family members, pastor or a member from the pastoral staff,
employer, social friends, or others who are meaningful in the individual's life. A good-sized intervention team is six to eight people.
Less than this number may lessen the impact; whereas, a larger
number of people may lessen the intimacy desired in the meeting.

The intervention should be held at a place where there will be
no interruptions. The pastor or counselor's office may be better
than the home because there would be fewer distractions. The
intervention must be at a time when the dependent person has a
sober mind.

One of the most difficult questions may be: How do we get the
dependent person to the pastor or counselor's office? I worked with
a dependent high school student after he overdosed on drugs over
a weekend. In planning for the intervention, the parents told the
son they had a meeting planned for him and themselves with me to
discuss ways they could help him and the family. The concerned
persons should not lie to the individual but insist on attendance at

the pastor's or counselor's office and continue until the person responds. After a significant event in life such as an arrest, traffic accident, threatened loss of job, or loss of a friend, the dependent person may be more willing to meet. After all, the person probably knows something is going on because family members have reduced their enabling behavior.

A preintervention rehearsal with the team will help prepare them for the event. Since participants may experience fear and an uneasiness about the meeting, a rehearsal will help them gain a sense of direction. Each concerned person should be prepared to give written data listing specific dates and events that document the dependent person's powerlessness over an addiction and the concerned person's feelings. The data should not refer to terms such as *dependency, addiction, alcoholic, or drug addict*; instead, let the facts speak for themselves. (Team members should understand that data documenting child abuse must be reported to proper authorities as required by law.) The rehearsal should close with a summarization and with prayer for God's guidance.

Once the actual intervention begins, the interventionist should explain that all present should hold their questions until each concerned person's data is shared. If the dependent person seeks to sidetrack the data, the interventionist should ask the person to wait until all have shared their concerns. It is important that the data be presented with love and compassion. The information should directly show how the dependent person's behavior affects each of the concerned persons.

After the data is presented, alternatives such as treatment programs or support groups should be presented. It is important that the team has already made arrangements with appropriate alternatives to insure that the dependent person can go for help immediately. The team should be prepared to follow up because the process of recovery has just started.

It should be made clear that if the dependent person leaves the room or refuses to receive help, the family members, pastor, employer, and others who may be on the team will continue to pray for recovery but will no longer offer support until the person chooses to change directions. They are letting the person go, trusting God to get his or her attention.

Relapse

A person who is recovering from a life-controlling problem should always be aware of the possibility of relapse into former ways. The writer of Proverbs says, "As a dog returns to its vomit, so a fool repeats his folly" (26:11). This is particularly true of those who are prone to extreme emotional highs and lows in their walk with God. Some may be overconfident in their recovery process to the point of not guarding against relapse. Crisis situations may trigger a person into relapse. Hidden fear or repressed anger may also lead to relapse.

Goals of Aftercare

Help for a person who is recovering from a life-controlling problem should focus on a vital relationship with God, freedom from the problems that have mastered his/her life, and personal self-esteem. Focusing on a person's relationship with God is a top priority in the individual's recovery.

Sobriety and sober thinking certainly must occur; however, this alone is not enough. Without an ongoing relationship with God, a person is likely to switch addictions. For example, Sam has been abstinent from alcohol for six months. However, his introduction to a higher power was void of a personal walk with Christ. Although he was abstaining from alcohol, he switched his dependency to ungodly sexual behaviors. Jesus deals with the principle of an unoccupied spiritual house in Matthew 12:43-45.

> When an evil spirit comes out of a man, it goes through arid places seeking rest and does not find it. Then it says, "I will return to the house I left." When it arrives, it finds the house unoccupied, swept clean and put in order. Then it goes and takes with it seven other

spirits more wicked than itself, and they go in and live there.

In addition to an active relationship with God, there must be continued abstinence or freedom from the life-controlling problem. A person who continues to drink alcohol, use drugs, or view R- and X-rated movies (or whatever the dependency is) cannot expect to remain in recovery. Fellowship with God will become strained as delusion once again dominates thinking.

Self-esteem is directly related to the person's relationship with God and personal abstinence or freedom from the problem that has mastered his/her life. Since God is perfect, He is the only one who can communicate personal significance to the person in recovery. Helpers should emphasize the self-worth that comes from being in Christ (*see* 1 Corinthians 1:30; Ephesians 1:3-14; Philippians 1:6, 4:13; Colossians 3:3). Paul writes: "In the same way, count yourselves dead to sin but alive to God in Christ Jesus" (Romans 6:11).

A feeling of being no good or of having no competence can be a difficult burden for a person struggling on the road to recovery. The helper can encourage the discouraged by helping the person understand that competence comes from a greater power. Paul writes: "Such confidence as this is ours through Christ before God. Not that we are competent to claim anything for ourselves, but our competence comes from God" (2 Corinthians 3:4-5).

A person's self-worth will suffer if he or she relapses into a former lifestyle. Since former values will be in conflict with new goals and lifestyle, feelings of failure and difficulty forgiving self will soon surface.

Ways to Attain Goals

An atmosphere of surrender should be encouraged whether it be in a group setting or one-on-one. Individuals who suffer from dependency should be encouraged to live their lives one day at a time (*see* Matthew 6:33-34). Honesty with themselves, God, and others helps prevent the growth of delusion. They should be encouraged to deal with their feelings and defenses. The helper should encourage persons dealing with relapse to communicate openly with God, asking for His forgiveness. "But if anybody does sin, we have one who speaks to the Father in our defense—Jesus Christ, the Righteous One"(1 John 2:1). An attitude of humility and responsibility to a local church body that holds the dependent accountable for recovery is an essential element in a recovery program.

Being aware of the various triggering devices that lead to relapse can be helpful to the person in recovery. Paul writes in 2 Corinthians 2:10-11: "I have forgiven in the sight of Christ for your sake, in order that Satan might not outwit us. For we are not unaware of his schemes." The helper should encourage the person to take a personal inventory of past experiences that enabled the use of a substance or practice to become a mastering behavior. For example, some people are tempted to relapse at times of celebration while others are more likely to fall during times of depression or stress. It is possible that the presence (or absence) of certain people, odors, music, or visual stimulation may contribute to a setback. A person should be aware of these devices and prayerfully take precautions against those things that may trigger a relapse.

Relapse Symptoms

A person who covers up an urge to relapse into a former lifestyle will probably begin to display observable negative behavior and return to the former state of denial. A first step is to start missing church services or support group meetings. When I was working in high schools with students who were chemically dependent, there was one sign exhibited by all who relapsed. They would immediately begin to avoid me in the hallways, cafeteria, or at ball games. They would also begin to drop out of their support group.

Socializing with the *former crowd* is another strong sign of relapse. An individual cannot stay straight and continue to *hang out* with former friends who project a negative influence. Being influenced by negative peer pressure will cause a gradual withdrawal from church and support group friends although some persons will continue to *talk the talk* but not *walk the walk*.

Ways to Deal with Relapse

It is important to keep communication lines open with those who have relapsed. In an effort to prevent delusion from growing, I would make eye and verbal contact with students who tried to avoid me. Practicing tough love, I would go to their homes when they skipped school and their support group meetings. I would level with them about observable behaviors that concerned me along with supporting data and specific dates.

A person who has relapsed should be encouraged to share feelings about the urge to use a substance or practice a mastering behavior. Encourage the person to continue work on recovery in a local church small group that can offer support and accountability. The helper should set goals of recovery and establish responsibility for meeting them.

Eight Core Conditions of Helping

In his adaptation of Robert Carkhuff's work, Gary Sweeten in his work, *Apples of Gold I* and *II*, shows eight qualities that are necessary for any person to be effective in helping relationships. When used successfully, these core conditions can benefit all relationships. These qualities are a process which requires practice. Local church helpers can have great tools, but without proper interpersonal skills, their success will be limited. A church may choose to put big dollars into various models and programs, but it will fail without proper people skills. These skills are centered on a person's tongue: "The tongue has the power of life and death" (Proverbs 18:21).

Accurate empathy. It is important to know the difference between empathy and sympathy. A person with accurate empathy can correctly perceive the feelings of another person without being captured by the victim's emotions. A person with sympathy actually feels what the victim feels, and this may prevent him from being objective in a helping relationship since he is likely to be *caught up* in the victim's emotions.

The key to accurate empathy is understanding the pain while remaining in a neutral position. The helper's goal should be to feel *with* the hurting person versus feeling *what* the individual feels. Whenever the helper and the seeker are experiencing the same feelings of pain, the focus may become pity and prevent the healing. Compassion and understanding assist the helper in perceiving the other person's feelings and experiences accurately.

One can be effective in helping a hurting person even though he or she may not be able to identify with the problem. A popular myth is a person must be a former drug user before he or she can help a victim of drug abuse. Jesus was effective in helping the hurting, yet he was sinless.

It is true that a divorcee can relate to another divorcee or a recovering addict can relate to a person caught in the web of an addiction. With accurate empathy, however, a person who has not experienced the same hurts can also be effective. The helping relationship starts with the development of trust and accurate empathy. "Two skills that appear to be easily taught to paraprofessional counselors are empathy and basic skills in cognitive behavior therapy" (Benner, 89).

Warmth. Warmth is communicated primarily through nonverbal ways including eye contact, nonpossessive touch, and body language. A congregation that has warmth will be accepting and caring instead of ignoring, rejecting, or giving a cold shoulder. Warmth is shown by a person's concern and affection for others.

People's inner feelings are often displayed by their tone of voice or body movement. A warm voice and a caring touch can bring peace and calmness to a brokenhearted person. Warmth communicates openness and thus lessens the defensiveness of a person seeking assistance and helps to build a trust relationship. Paul states in Romans 12:10 (PHILLIPS), "Let us have real warm affection for one another as between brothers, and a willingness to let the other man have the credit." Warmth is nonverbal openness which helps create an environment for healing and growth in the local church.

Respect. People with this quality display *agape* love which accepts a person as he or she is. They treat other people as equals and do not put them down. Having respect for another person does not mean the helper takes ownership of the problems or rescues them from responsibilities.

This quality in a helper separates a person from his or her behavior and looks beyond the sin and sees the person as being created by God. A genuine interest is shown in the person with the life-controlling problem. This kind of interest does not always provide quick answers but gives the person seeking help space to gain personal insight. The helper respects the topics initiated by the person seeking help and does not try to divert attention to the helper's interests. A person shows respect by understanding limitations and time restraints. There may be times when the helper must refer a person to someone else for help thus displaying respect for the individual. Every person, regardless of social or moral status, deserves respect as a human being. "Show proper respect to everyone" (1 Peter 2:17).

Genuineness. A genuine person is not a phony and does not play the role of superiority. He or she is truthful, honest about feelings, and does not wear a mask which presents a false image. Paul's genuineness is described in 1 Thessalonians 2:5: "You know we never used flattery, nor did we put on a mask to cover up greed—God is our witness." Being genuine does not mean a person is so transparent that he or she hurts or offends people with honesty.

This quality presents a good role model. This person is consistent from day to day and does not live two lives. A genuine person does not get caught up in fads just to please others. The best example of genuineness is Jesus Christ. Paul says Jesus "made himself nothing,

taking the very nature of a servant, being made in human likeness"
(Philippians 2:7). A genuine person's inner feelings are consistent
with words and deeds. "Genuineness implies spontaneity without
impulsiveness and honesty without cruel confrontation. It means
that the helper is deeply himself or herself—not thinking or feeling
one thing and saying something different" (Collins, 25, 1980). A
genuine person is an open individual who has nothing to prove.

Self-disclosure. A helper can share his or her own personal experiences and insight that may assist the seeker in understanding how
to deal with a life-controlling problem. A helper should use caution
and not overuse self-disclosure by talking too much thereby shifting
the focus of the conversation away from the seeker.

The helper should have a clear goal for self-disclosing. Self-disclosure should not be confused with empathy which seeks to "feel
with" the person. The goal is to provide insight the person seeking
help does not appear to have. While sharing with the individual,
the helper should not talk down to the seeker as being inferior or
as a child; rather, the person should be treated as an adult talking
to another adult. Sharing insights for the purpose of helping
should always be positive in conversation although the outcome
may be painful. "God is not the *Author* of all events, but He is the
Master of all events" (Seamands, 139). Stay at the level of insight
relevant to the person's need. "Admit your faults to one another
and pray for each other so that you may be healed" (James 5:16
TLB). Self-disclosure should be for the purpose of bringing healing
to the person enslaved by a stronghold.

Concreteness. This quality is used to help move a person from the
generalities of a discussion to the specific areas of need. It is common for an individual with a life-controlling problem to provide the
presenting problem before giving the real problem. The truth
often comes in bits and pieces before all the facts are assembled.
Gary Sweeten in his work on the eight core conditions of helping
states:

> There are some basic principles which come through the Scripture
> in a very consistent manner. One of those principles is this: be sure
> to take all the facts into consideration prior to deciding a major

course of action (this implies using concreteness). There are numerous proof texts to support the conclusion that concreteness is important. . . .

There are some who believe that living by faith demands that we ignore the facts of life. However, Biblical faith enables us to look squarely at the facts and yet have faith in God's deliverance, mercy, and power (66).

Andrew presented the facts to Jesus in regard to feeding the 5,000. "Here is a boy with five small barley loaves and two small fish, but how far will they go among so many" (John 6:9)? Jesus did not ignore the facts, nor did he rebuke Andrew for his lack of faith. He simply responded to the specific facts and "took the loaves, gave thanks, and distributed to those who were seated as much as they wanted. He did the same with the fish" (John 6:11). Jesus acted on the facts he received from Andrew.

Confrontation. It is no accident that this quality is listed near the end of the eight core conditions of helping. There must be a display of the previous conditions such as empathy, warmth, and respect before a relationship can benefit from confrontation. Careful confrontation can be helpful in bringing about action and accountability after the helper has won the right to be heard.

The helper must be careful not to be harsh in his confrontation of a person who has a life-controlling problem. "Brothers, if someone is caught in a sin, you who are spiritual should restore him gently. But watch yourself, or you also may be tempted" (Galatians 6:1). Confrontation should not be used as a means of power or control. It should be done with sensitivity with the purpose of helping the person break out of delusion and grow in Christ.

Immediate feedback. Focusing on the health of the relationship, this quality deals with the immediate relationship between two people. Immediate feedback cannot be effective without regular use of the other core conditions. This quality represents understanding of each other, warm acceptance, dealing with specifics, genuineness, reflection on each other's feelings, and confrontation when necessary.

Immediate feedback is necessary to prevent walls from being built in a relationship. This helps individuals keep in touch with possible delusions that could develop. Paul worked hard to prevent walls from being built between himself and others. "Even if I caused you sorrow by my letter, I do not regret it. Though I did regret it— I see that my letter hurt you, but only for a little while—yet now I am happy, not because you were made sorry, but because your sorrow led you to repentance" (2 Corinthians 7:8-9).

Family Emotional Stages

Elisabeth Kübler-Ross in her book, *On Death and Dying*, describes a five-step process that dying people experience in accepting their death: *denial, anger, bargaining, depression,* and *acceptance.* A family who has one of its members affected by a life-controlling problem will experience the same process.

According to mental health professionals, people experience these stages whenever there is any loss, major or minor. They may go through the stages as listed, or they may jump back and forth from one to another. Although he was physically alive, the prodigal son's father recognized his son as being dead. "For this son of mine was dead and is alive again" (Luke 15:24).

Denial

Sue was surprised when she received a call from the police telling her that her daughter had been arrested at the shopping mall for shoplifting. She denied that Jennifer could do this because she had everything a sixteen-year-old girl could want. The family lived in the nicest area in the city, had a swimming pool in their backyard, membership to the country club, and Jennifer had her own sports car.

Sue refused to accept the reality that Jennifer was a shoplifter. She said, "There must be a mistake; Jennifer would not do such a thing. Besides, taking a $10 bracelet is no big deal! After all, girls go through these stages when they sow their wild oats." Sue felt she was in control of Jennifer and could shield her from future problems. She used denial to help herself with the shock and for protection from reality.

To help a person in denial, the helper should work to gain the denier's confidence. The person suffering from denial needs help in feeling safe to the point of taking a look at what is really happening. The helper needs to see that the victim is controlling his or her life and that denial distorts thinking.

Anger

While sitting in her office completing a business deal with a client one afternoon, Sue received a call from the high school principal. He asked her to come to the school immediately because Jennifer had stolen a wallet from one of the students. Sue became angry and cursed him on the telephone. She told the principal that the environment at the school contributed to drugs and stealing.

After thinking more about Jennifer, Sue became angry with God and herself. She blamed God for the problem. She angrily talked to God saying, "Why me, God? Why is this happening? Jennifer has everything a teenager could want."

Sue blamed herself. She said, "If I were a better person, Jennifer would not be getting into trouble." She blamed the church youth program for not having a good enough ministry to help Jennifer stay out of trouble.

It was common for Sue and Jennifer to get into physical fights. Sue called their minister and his wife to come to their house one evening after a fight. They noticed Sue was bruised and scratched and the banister to the stairway was broken from the altercation. Sue was in emotional pain, and her crying would not stop. After the fight, Jennifer got into her car and left in an emotional rage. Sue was concerned for Jennifer's safety and asked her minister for help.

A person in the anger stage needs help in seeing how his or her life is being controlled and preoccupied by the victim. Being aware of the anger and not permitting it to become a stronghold is important (*see* Ephesians 4:26-27). A person in the anger stage should be encouraged to share feelings. Helping the person to take a look at what the anger is doing to the marital relationship is also encouraged. The helper needs to be a good listener, remembering that the anger stage is normal.

Bargaining

Sue began to strike a bargain with herself, others, and God. She contracted with herself to be a better housekeeper and to lose 20 pounds within 60 days. She also struck a deal with Jennifer. She agreed to buy her a new car if she would refrain from shoplifting.

Deals were made with God on behalf of Jennifer. Sue promised to join the PTA if God would help Jennifer stop shoplifting. She also promised to teach a Sunday school class and increase her financial support of the church.

A person in this stage needs to understand that help for a friend or loved one does not depend on one's performance. None of us is good enough to merit God's help. "For all have sinned and fall short of the glory of God, and are justified freely by his grace through the redemption that came by Christ Jesus" (Romans 3:23-24). The helper should encourage the bargainer to look closely at our powerlessness to change another person.

Depression

In this stage, Sue began to experience extensive pain because she saw no hope for Jennifer. With reality setting in, she felt the pain of losing a child to shoplifting. Grief filled her life when she thought about her parental relationship to Jennifer. This time was particularly tough for Sue because she also felt the pain of a marriage to a passive husband and father to Jennifer. Melody Beattie in her work on the grief process states:

When we see our bargain has not worked, when we finally become exhausted from our struggle to ward off reality, and when we decide to acknowledge what life has socked to us we become sad, sometimes terribly depressed. This is the essence of grief: mourning at its fullest. This is what we have been attempting at all costs to avoid. This is the time to cry, and it hurts. This stage of the process begins when we humbly surrender, says Esther Olson, a family counselor who works with the grief, or as she calls it, "forgiveness process." It will disappear, she says, only when the process has been worked out and through (124-125).

Depression is generally brought on by the loss of something or someone. Reacting to a loss is normal in the grief process. Archibald Hart states:

When a normal depression doesn't remit within a reasonable period of time (at the longest two weeks) then it becomes a clinical depression and should be treated . . . it is possible for a psychologically triggered depression to be just as painful and serious in its symptoms as any biologically based depression (48, 1987).

A person in this stage needs hope and help in understanding his feelings. The helper should encourage the depressed person to share emotions. David repeatedly reports his experience with grief in the Book of Psalms. The sharing of painful emotions helps one work through the depression stage. Paul writes: "Praise be to the God and Father of our Lord Jesus Christ, the Father of compassion and the God of all comfort, who comforts us in all our troubles, so that we can comfort those in any trouble with the comfort we ourselves have received from God" (2 Corinthians. 1:3-4).

Acceptance

Sue set an appointment to see her minister. She explained to him that Jennifer was also drinking alcohol and had stolen $2,000 from

Sue's checking account. She said, "I've had all I can take. I have given her back to God." At the suggestion of the minister, Jennifer eventually agreed to enter a Christian treatment program where she received help for her deviant behavior.

At the acceptance stage a person feels free to turn a friend or loved one over to God. This does not mean the person condones or takes pleasure in what is happening in the victim's life; instead, the reality of the situation has been accepted. This is a time when the wounded emotionally detach themselves from the one they love so much. If the victim gets help, the persons in the acceptance stage do not feel they have to receive the credit. They have accepted their powerlessness to change another person. Paul writes in Romans 7:18: "I know that nothing good lives in me, that is, in my sinful nature. For I have the desire to do what is good, but I cannot carry it out."

The mother of Moses recognized her powerlessness to spare him from Pharaoh's decree which called for each baby boy to be thrown into the Nile River. When she could no longer hide the baby, she prepared a basket and placed him in it among the reeds on the river bank. As the sister of Moses watched, Pharaoh's daughter found the baby, spared the child, and helped him grow into adulthood. Moses became a great deliverer because his mother was willing to turn him over to God.

It is extremely important for a helping person to understand the grief process. Without this understanding, a helper may give up when a person denies he or she has a problem. It may appear that the victim does not want your help or is just indifferent. If you as a helping person understand the grief process, you are not likely to take the victim's anger personally and bow out of the helping relationship.

Helping individuals who are experiencing hurt behind their Sunday smiles begins with an environment of acceptance and love. Practicing the eight core conditions of helping along with carefronting sets the tone for an environment of healing and growth. A person is most likely to level in this type of atmosphere. This helps individuals to face the reality of their need for God's help which is always the first step of recovery from a life-controlling problem or a relapse.

7

Family Systems

The family has become so fragmented that it is difficult to describe a normal family in this addictive society. The traditional family was once the core foundation and stabilizing force of our society. Now, many special interest groups, sociology professors, and even marriage counselors who do not have a clue as to what "family values" mean are giving advice to families. According to University of Pennsylvania psychologist, Martin Seligman, "past generations were able to maintain hope through difficult times because they had three anchors of stability in all of their societies: faith in God, pride in one's country, and stability in the family" (Collins and Clinton, 51).

When we consider that almost every one out of every two marriages will end in divorce and the children will see this example of pain and failure, it is not surprising that today's baby boomers, busters, and Generation Xers have difficulty seeing marriage as a trust institution. Collins and Clinton in their work, *Baby Boomer Blues*, quote Neil Kalter: "There is mounting evidence now that a substantial number of children, perhaps as many as 30 to 50 percent, bear the painful and disruptive legacy of their parents' divorce for years" (62).

In the minds of many people, having children without being married, homosexual marriages, and having sexual relationships outside of marriage are fine if that is one's belief system. The breakdown of the family is cradled in moral erosion. In a society where there are no boundaries, the definition of morality develops into whatever fits the situation. Without a foundation of biblical principles, husbands and wives have difficulty understanding each other because the male and female role differences become blurred. "Communication problems are the number one reason for divorce in the 1990's. As we found out, women don't really understand men, and men don't really understand women" (Patterson and Kim, 91).

The breakdown of the family is largely responsible for this addictive society. The term "for better or worse" is more likely interpreted, "if you make me feel good and meet my needs"—centered on self.

How amazing it is to live in a day when most young people expect marriages to dissolve; when a large and growing percentage of babies are born to single mothers; when cohabitation and sexual intercourse before marriage are assumed to be normal, moral and rational behaviors; and when one out of four adults accepts homosexual couples as viable parents (Barna, 143).

William J. Bennett in his book, *The Index of Leading Cultural Indicators*, which is based on facts and figures on the state of American society, presents alarming information. He says that since 1960, violent crime has increased by 560 percent, the number of unmarried pregnant teenagers has nearly doubled, and the number of divorces has increased by nearly 200 percent while the marriage rate is at an all-time low. James Q. Wilson, University of California, Los Angeles, says:

The contemporary legal system views people as autonomous individuals endowed with rights and entering into real or implied contracts. The liberalization of laws pertaining to marriage and divorce arose out of such a view. Marriage, once a sacrament, has become in the eyes of the law a contract that is easily negotiated, renegotiated or rescinded (Bennett, 57).

In Wilson's statement, there are two interesting thoughts: "autonomous individuals" and "marriage, once a sacrament." He deals with two key factors in this addictive society—individualism and separation from God. Selfishness, the refusal to acknowledge God, and marriage no longer being a sacrament can only lead individuals in this society to pursue themselves as god.

With today's maze of family life, we are much like a dog chasing its own tail—going in circles and becoming more confused and sick. People in government are crying for more money, communities call for public forums, and some church leaders offer theories and fine-sounding arguments with little substance. Many such leaders are truly concerned but often base their thoughts on their own dysfunctional "frame of thought."

I have heard many fathers and mothers say, "I really want to be a good dad, mom, husband, or wife; however, I am not sure how—I did not have a role model." With family fragmentation, busy lifestyles, relocations, and an increase in second and third marriages, we have lost much of the continuity with the past we once had. In the past when we needed marriage or career counseling, we went to grandma. Long before there were psychologists, there were grandmas.

There is no way we can turn around this devastation of family life and its consequences in our society without first understanding God's plan for marriage and family relationships. We cannot change what we cannot see. The term "one flesh" and its meaning in the marriage relationship is foreign to most people. Concerning "one flesh," Richard Halverson said:

Their biological diversity was to be their unity, and out of the most intimate relationship humans experience came the creative power to beget life. Which is part of the image of God in man. So called "sexual freedom" violates sexuality—mars the image of God in man—degrades human nature . . . and destroys the social order. "Sexual freedom" is the final stage in man's self-alienation from God (July 17, 1991, 1).

In this chapter, we are going to trace God's plan for marriage and family relationships. To understand marriage properly, we will first look at its beginning and foundation. Genesis 2:22-24 presents to us the first marriage:

> Then the LORD God made a woman from the rib he had taken out of the man, and he brought her to the man. The man said, 'This is now bone of my bones and flesh of my flesh; she shall be called woman, for she was taken out of man.' For this reason a man will leave his father and mother and be united to his wife, and they will become one flesh.

The first marriage was a paradigm built on a foundation of five principles. First, God is the creator of the marriage relationship (vv22-24). This relationship was not dreamed up by a sociologist or psychologist, nor did it occur because of a consensus reached through a poll. Instead, God said, "It is not good for the man to be alone. I will make a helper suitable for him" (Genesis 2:18).

Second, heterosexuality is God's pattern for marriage. Adam was male and Eve was female (v23; Genesis 3:20; Leviticus 18:22). It is a distortion of Scripture to proclaim homosexuality as an accepted behavior in the Bible. "Those who attempt to mount a biblical case for homosexuality must completely abandon reasonable hermeneutics" (Davis, 78).

Third, monogamy is God's design for marriage. God gave Adam one wife (vv22-24; 4:1; Hebrews 13:4). Sex outside of marriage causes physical, emotional, and spiritual problems.

Fourth, God's pattern for marriage is for physical and spiritual unity (v24; Matthew 19:4-5). God describes this union as "one flesh." They are to cleave to one another, literally to be glued to each other. When two are pulled apart who were glued together, it will leave a mess as divorce does. "Marriage is an exclusive relationship. The total unity of persons—physically, emotionally, intellectually, and spiritually—comprehended by the concept one flesh eliminates polygamy as an option. One cannot relate wholeheartedly in this way to more than one person at a time" (Elwell, 694).

And fifth, God's first marriage was designed to be permanent (v24). In Matthew 19:6, Jesus referred back to the first marriage. "So they are no longer two, but one. Therefore, what God has joined together, let man not separate." In this union, adultery, homosexuality, and promiscuity are ruled out of this holy pattern. "God instituted marriage so that men and women might complete one another and share in his creative work through the procreation of children. (Celibacy is not a higher and holier condition—a viewpoint which finds its roots in Greek dualism rather than in the Bible)" (Elwell, 694).

As we trace God's plan for marriage and the family, we see its significant role in the Ten Commandments. The Israelites had been delivered from slavery in Egypt and were enroute to the promised land when God dealt with the first of the commandments that zeroes in on social relationships. This is the first of His commandments on human interaction. This shows God's priority on the foundation of all human relationships—the family. "Honor your father and your mother, so that you may live long in the land the LORD your God is giving you" (Exodus 20:12).

This commandment is the centerpiece of all the commandments. The first four commandments deal with our relationship with God; whereas, the last six commandments focus on social relationships. This commandment serves as a bridge from our focus on God to our focus on interpersonal relationships. If the first four commandments are obeyed, the following six will be less difficult. If the focus on God is not present in the home, social relationships in all of society including church, school, our nation, and employer/employee relationships will suffer for lack of respect, direction, and purpose. Rules will change frequently without an anchor, and subsequent ethical decisions become the product of frail and flawed humanity.

In God's pattern, honoring one's father and mother is a model of respect for God and others. Honor is learned in the home and flows into other areas of respect for various kinds of authority.

> The family forms the foundation of all human relationships. This principle has, of course, been demonstrated also in the behavioral sciences. Psychologists have made a great deal (I would argue, too much) of the determinative character of our families. Those who are abused in that environment themselves often abuse; whereas, those who come from strong, loving, and supportive backgrounds are less likely to commit the crimes associated with the rest of the Ten Commandments that follow (M. Horton, 136).

As we look at today's family life, there are various kinds of family paradigms that are common in this society. A family system is the attitudes and patterns by which a family operates over a period of three generations and is characterized by each family member being a part of the whole. In observing one's family system, a person should picture himself or herself as one part of the whole family unit. When a family member has a life-controlling problem, others in the family will operate normally within their family system experience to resolve the problem.

The Dysfunctional Family

Dysfunctional families are a tragic and growing part of our society. This specific type of family is the one in which the authority line between the parents and children is blurry. In this family, it is hard to detect who is in charge. Teenagers make decisions in regard to their well-being that should be made by their parents. Sixteen-year-old Mike was permitted to drink alcohol because his parents thought he needed his space to make his own decisions. He was involved with other teenagers who were a bad influence, but the parents would not interfere with Mike's decision.

In this type of family, the parents live for and compete for the children. They learn to live their lives vicariously through their children. Some fathers may press their sons to excel in sports because they were never successful themselves. Having an unfulfilled desire to march in front of the high school or college band, some mothers may push their daughters to be outstanding majorettes. The parents blame each other for problems they encounter. They put on a good front for others and maintain a supply of defenses to cover up their behavior.

It is common for coalitions to develop with one of the parents working as an enabler to the child with deviant behavior. The other parent may have close ties to the child that is *straight*. If there are other children, they may not be a part of either coalition. The emotions between the parents are broken down, and they may relate to the children better than to each other.

In an attempt to maintain family stability, some parents may use another person or object to prevent the son or daughter with a life-controlling problem from exploding the family relationship. Triangles are common in dysfunctional families. A parent may sit with a *problem child* in a room where the television set is the third leg of the triangle. Their focus will be on the television program instead of dealing with the problem. Parents may focus on the son or daughter with a life-controlling problem in a triangle relationship to avoid issues among themselves. Triangles serve to break down communications and prolong the agony of a dysfunctional family.

In some dysfunctional families, there are patterns of permissive parenting and neglectful parenting. The permissive parenting model usually has few boundaries or controls but is supportive. They tend to allow their children to make their own rules. In their view, to interrupt with firm guidance could cause harm to the child's creative mind. Neglectful parenting produces "latchkey children." They carry this label because they are in charge of the latchkey. They come and go as they please. They are left to make decisions without the support, guidance, or control of their parents. The children care for themselves.

The Disengaged Family

In this type of family there is a very strong authority line between the parents and children with very little going on emotionally. The boundaries in this family are rigid with a lack of communication. This family unit is characterized by one of the parents being legalistic or unyielding and the other parent being passive. The teenagers in this family normally go their own way.

Mary was dismayed when she found that her son was heavily involved in drugs. She was encouraged by a Christian friend to visit with a counselor. In her conversation with the counselor, she timidly discussed her son but with the understanding that the counselor would not tell her husband of the visit. She said, "If my husband learns of Joe's problem with drugs, he will hurt him." In this situation the counselor urged a meeting with both parents in order to reach a better understanding. He knew that in this type of family it often takes a family member's problem reaching a crisis point before the family responds.

The disengaged family is low on support but very strong on their rules and control. This family has many rules but without relationships. It is common in this family pattern for children to look forward to reaching adulthood so they can leave this domineering system.

The Functional Family

Judy was fortunate to be in a Christian family that had a solid family system. She was very excited about being asked to the prom by her boyfriend. Since this was a special evening, she asked her mom for permission to stay out beyond her scheduled curfew. Her mother, Polly, did not have a good reason to deny the request, but she felt in her heart that she should say no. She explained to Judy that she did not have a specific reason as to why the curfew should not be extended but she had a *gut feeling* that the curfew should be honored. Judy was supposed to leave the prom no later than 12 a.m.

Very upset with her mother, Judy went to her dad, Steve, seeking an intervention into Mom's decision. Steve and Polly stood together in their decision even though Judy persisted in her request. Finally, on the day of the prom, Polly in Steve's presence said to Judy, "Darling, we love you very much and we trust you; however, we do not feel good about changing the curfew."

Throughout the evening after Judy left for the prom, Steve and Polly pondered their decision and hoped that Judy would respect the curfew even though she was upset. Steve and Polly were delighted to hear the door open at the specified time. Judy had obeyed her parents and honored the curfew.

Later that morning as Judy was asleep in her bed, four teenagers were killed in a car accident. The same car Judy would have been riding in had she chosen to break the curfew skidded off the rain-slick road, went down an embankment, and hit a tree. The teenagers in the car were killed and not found until some time later in the morning. Thinking that Judy was in the wreck, Steve and Polly's neighbors were terribly shaken. When Judy and her parents returned home from church on that Sunday morning, some of the neighbors began to weep for joy when they saw her and thanked God that she was not in the accident.

Communication lines are open between the parents and children in this type of family system. Children have input into family matters; however, the parents make the final decision in regard to the child's well-being. Steve and Polly listened to Judy's request for an extension of the curfew on prom night, but they felt it was in the best interest of Judy for them not to extend it.

This family unit is characterized by a sense of family wholeness. Each family member has a feeling of belonging which contributes to their personal self-esteem. This is an open system where friends can be invited into the home without the family's feeling they must protect themselves.

The characteristics of a functional family are described by Paul in Ephesians 5:21-6:4. Each family member has a role to play in God's plan for the family. This unit functions properly when there is submission to Christ. Husband and wife are admonished to stand together as one in Christ. "For this reason a man will leave his father and mother and be united to his wife, and the two will become one flesh"(5:31). Even though Judy tried to convince her father that he should side with her and permit the curfew extension, Steve stood with Polly in her decision.

Paul describes checks and balances to prevent abuse and neglect in the family unit. The entire unit operates under the lordship of Jesus Christ. In the functional family, parents are male and female, not two of the same sex cohabiting together. Wives are to submit to their husbands, but husbands are admonished to love their wives. "Husbands, love your wives, just as Christ loved the church and gave himself up for her" (5:25). This is a strong check for husbands with no room for abuse or neglect of the wife.

Children are to grow under the *godly covering* of their parents. "Children, obey your parents in the Lord, for this is right. 'Honor your father and mother'—which is the first commandment with a promise" (6:1-2). Even though she disliked it, Judy honored her parents' decision, recognizing their authority (*godly covering*).

Children need to see a loving relationship between their parents. Spouses who love and respect each other contribute greatly to the children's sense of well-being. Children face far less emotional problems when parents are affectionate toward one another. It helps prepare the children emotionally for personal relationships and marriage. Parents who openly express their appreciation for each other enhance their children's sense of security.

Much attention has been given to children in this country. This has caused us to become a child-centered society. Certainly children need our attention; however, parents must guard against the love of the family being focused solely on the children. Such a focus can cause the disintegration of the marriage over a period of time. When children become the center of family love, the love affair between the mom and dad may grow cold. When the children grow up and leave home, the parents may face difficulty in staying together because the flame has disappeared.

Diana Baumrind (1967, 1978) identified three types of parents—authoritative, authoritarian, and permissive. She found that a combination of high levels of control and support, a style which she called "authoritative," is most conducive to developing competency in children. She suggested that an authoritarian style (low support and high control) produces children who have a respect for authority, but show little independence and only moderate social competence. Permissive parenting (high support and low control) tends to produce children who lack both social competence and interdependence (Balswick and Balswick, 95).

In view of Baumrind's work, we define her term "authoritative" as the functional pattern we discussed. In this system there are high levels of control and support. The authoritarian style we define as disengaged and permissive parenting as dysfunctional. It is dysfunctional because it produces unhealthy families.

The Ephesians 5:21-6:4 passage provides practical guidelines for each role in the marriage and family relationships. The key verse is verse 21. "Submit to one another out of reverence for Christ." This is a bridge verse between the Spirit-filled life discussed in verses 18-20 and the guidelines in verses 22-6:4. Paul shows how to take a Spirit-filled life and move it into the practical relationships of everyday living. It is noteworthy that other social relationships discussed in Ephesians 6:5-9, employee and employer, flow from the home as already discussed in the Ten Commandments.

To summarize this section of practical relationships, we conclude that Paul addresses wives to husbands (5:22-24), husbands to wives (5:25-33), children to parents (6:1-3), parents to children (6:4), employees to employers (6:5-8), and employers to employees (6:9). This will work if we will let it work.

Christ and the Church: The Model for Marriage

In the Ephesians 5:22-33 passage, we also see the Apostle Paul presenting Christ and the Church as a pattern for marriage. God shows the importance and high standing of marriage by using Christ and the Church as a pattern to follow.

I have heard some say they know of marriages that are very functional and neither the husband nor the wife are Christians. It can also be said that there are many Christian husbands and wives whose marriages are far from being an example to follow. How can this be explained? Even partners in marriages who do not profess Christianity but follow many of the principles in the Ephesians passage will have success. On the other hand, many Christian husbands and wives are hampered by marital strife because one wants to follow God's plan while the other seems unconcerned.

As we look at Christ and the Church as the model for marriage, the principles involved will take Christian marriages to another plane of living. A Spirit-filled marriage, a marriage that is under the control of the Holy Spirit, that follows the guidelines in the Ephesians passage, will become a miracle relationship. They will experience marriage as "the best thing this side of heaven." A Spirit-filled marriage is more than exercising spiritual gifts or having Scripture verses plastered on the walls of our house. It is having a life where the husband and wife have a daily walk with Christ in prayer, meditation, and Bible reading—communion with God and with each other.

Jack and Judith Balswick have a good understanding of family relationships. They suggest "a theology of family relationships which involves four sequential, but nonlinear stages: covenant, grace, empowering and intimacy" (21). In each part of these four cornerstones of marriage there are principles that clearly show Christ and the Church as an example for a marriage that will grow and not stagnate. First, it is built on an agreement that is a covenant, not a contract. Christ's relationship to the Church is a covenant relationship. "Christ is the mediator of a new covenant" (Hebrews 9:15). The Balswicks describe the covenant in marriage as an "unconditional commitment" (24). God's love is unconditional; therefore, ours should be also.

Second, the atmosphere in the marriage is grace. Christ was "full of grace and truth" (John 1:14). Forgiveness is a characteristic of this atmosphere. If the marriage is built on a covenant agreement, then the atmosphere is one of grace. However, if the marriage is built on a contract agreement, it will become an atmosphere of law. In an atmosphere of grace, we will practice our family roles in Ephesians 5:21-6:4 because we want to, not because we have to. "In an atmosphere of grace family members act responsibly out of love and consideration for one another" (Balswick and Balswick, 26).

Next, in this marriage built on a covenant agreement with an atmosphere of grace, how will the marriage partners act in their relationship with one another? They will empower each other. Instead of being possessive, their goal will be to serve one another. Remember, our example is Christ and the Church. Jesus came to serve. He "did not come to be served, but to serve" (Matthew 20:28).

Serving and being served does not mean this family has no guidelines or firm love. The parents fulfill their position of authority by helping their children learn how to be responsible. "Empowering is the process of helping another recognize strengths and potentials within, as well as encouraging and guiding the development of these qualities" (Balswick and Balswick, 28). To serve one another is love in action.

With these cornerstones in a marriage—a covenant agreement, an atmosphere of grace, action of serving and being served—the association is intimacy. Instead of distance between the marriage partners, they are drawing closer and closer to each other. They know each other. The couple is truly "one flesh." 1 John 4:18-19 shows this kind of love and intimacy. "There is no fear in love. But perfect love drives out fear, because fear has to do with punishment. The man who fears is not made perfect in love. We love because he first loved us." In this marriage the partners are free to share with one another. There are no hidden agendas.

This family relationship can be the best thing this side of heaven. It does not happen overnight but is an ever-growing process.

> Intimacy can lead to deeper covenant love, commitment fortifies the atmosphere of freely offered grace, this climate of acceptance and forgiveness encourages serving and empowering others, and the resultant sense of esteem leads to the ability to be intimate without fear (Balswick and Balswick, 33).

Family Challenges

" 'I hate divorce', says the LORD God of Israel" (Malachi 2:16). God hates divorce but loves those who have experienced divorce. It is not surprising that God hates divorce because of all the pain and suffering that divorcees and their families experience. The effects of divorce cause psychological problems on both parents and children for years. With the high rate of divorce and fragmentation, families are faced with complex and difficult systems with which to work. Some of the more common units are single parents and blended families.

Single Parents

Single-parent homes are not necessarily dysfunctional. The authority lines already described in the dysfunctional, disengaged, and functional system are the same except there is only one parent instead of two. The single-parent home can be functional when the communication lines are open with the children. As in two-parent homes, the single parent is encouraged to make the final decision in regard to the children's well-being. Sometimes the single parent is helped in a desire for a functional family by children who notice a mom's or dad's hard work in caring for the family.

Although single-parent families can function in an effective way, the challenges can be enormous. Lack of financial resources causes pressure, and the lack of community often causes such families to feel isolated. These pressures can be very discouraging to single-parent families and can be the cause for depression. The local church should be the extended family for the single-parent home. Married couples need to include single parents in their social and ministry activities in the local church.

Blended Family

About 80 percent of the people who divorce from their first spouse will remarry. A blended family is a family with at least one child in the household from a previous marriage. There are several factors that will need to be addressed in a blended family, some of which are to redefine the meaning of father and mother, boundaries, the children's uncertainties toward their role, and their relationship with the absent birth parent.

Dr. Raymond T. Brock in his work, *Parenting the Elementary Child*, has done extensive work in the area of "blended families." He states that "it is difficult to call two men 'father' or two women 'mother,' when this involves the comparison between a birth parent and a stepparent. . . . The child should be given a choice in selecting the name he or she will call the new parent" (58). The child should not be forced to call the new parent mom or dad. The new parent will need to earn the trust of the child or children. This takes time. The goal is not to replace the biological parent.

When a blended family comes together, clear boundaries should be established. Respect for each person in the family should be taught and modeled by the parents. "Rules must be clearly established for contact as well as distance regarding sexuality, conflict, and territory" (Brock, 59). Each person needs his or her own space. Respect for each family member's space and property should be clearly defined and upheld.

As children from a previous marriage enter into a blended family, they face the ambiguity of their role in the new family. This uncertainty of their role will usually bring anxiety, questions, and sometimes fear, particularly if the children have not been prepared. For example, in the previous marriage a child may have been the oldest in the family, but in the blended family he is the middle or even the youngest child. Each child will need time to adjust to their new role as it relates to birth order. Dr. Brock states that "responsibilities and privileges should be linked in a hierarchy that is constantly communicated" (Brock, 59).

Perhaps one of the most difficult and often uncomfortable challenges is the relationship with the absent birth parent. In the case of a divorce, there may have been strained and even bitter negotiations regarding the divorce settlement which placed the children in a difficult position. This is a state that no child deserves, but unfortunately, it happens all the time. In this case, both parents need to focus on the well-being of the child while trying to make the proceedings as painless as possible. "Children need to be taught that to give love to a new stepparent does not subtract love from the absent parent. It is not a matter of loss or disloyalty, it is a matter of enlargement of the heart" (Brock, 58).

Rebellious Children

Children should be taught they are accountable to God for their actions as the parents are responsible to be a godly covering for them. Solomon writes in Proverbs 1:8: "Listen, my son, to your father's instruction and do not forsake your mother's teaching." Children should be made aware of God's law of authority even though we live in a society that is unbalanced in its declaration of rights and responsibilities. Much emphasis is placed on personal rights but very little is said about being responsible for our own actions. Paul writes in Romans 13:1: "Everyone must submit himself to governing authorities, for there is no authority except that which God has established."

If children refuse to walk under their parental covering (authority), they should be taught there will always be another authority in line. However, the next first line of authority under God may not be as kind and caring as their parents. For example, if Johnny refuses to obey his godly (parental) covering and decides to use drugs, his authority may become a judge, prison, or hospital system.

Having a functional family system does not guarantee that children will never go astray. Children have choices to make also, and it is not right to always pin the blame on parents. Youth are instructed in Proverbs 4 to guard their hearts against the wicked. If children rebel, parents should keep the lines of communication open but hold their loved one accountable for his or her actions.

Paul warns fathers against the abuse and neglect of the children. "Fathers, do not exasperate your children; instead, bring them up in the training and instruction of the Lord" (Ephesians 6:4). The functional family is characterized by loving parents who serve as role models. Moses writes: "Only be careful, and watch yourselves closely so that you do not forget the things your eyes have seen or let them slip from your heart as long as you live. Teach them to your children and to the children after them" (Deuteronomy 4:9).

With the decline in role models in various walks of life including sports, religion, and politics, children desperately need to have parents who are good role models. "Don't do as I do, do as I say" is poor logic. Children will learn to pattern their behaviors based on what they see from their parents. Children in functional families will learn more from the values modeled by their parents versus those taught but not practiced.

Boundaries for children are established by the parents in the functional family. "Stay always within the boundaries where God's love can reach and bless you" (Jude 21 TLB). Young people will have more respect for established rules if there are open communications between the parents and children. If the boundaries are broken, then the youth should be held accountable for their actions.

Young people want boundaries. As they become older, young people often resent their parents for not providing these boundaries. These boundaries help to provide a "safety zone" for children. Sometimes the boundaries give them a good reason to say no when they may otherwise give in to negative peer pressure. I heard a seventeen-year-old high school student say, "I wish my father would ask me not to drink." After receiving help, another student who was chemically dependent thanked his parents for intervening in his addiction.

In the functional family, parents will know where their teenagers are and with whom they associate. They will find out the answers to such questions as, "Is alcohol served in the home where the teenager has been invited to attend a party?" "Will there be adult supervision?" "What time does the party end?" The parents will have a curfew and insist on its observance.

Children need help in dealing with negative peer pressure. Paul writes: "Do not be misled: 'Bad company corrupts good character'" (1 Corinthians 15:33). Peer pressure not only affects young people, but it can also influence parents. They may try to "keep up with the Joneses" or spend too much time with their peers and not enough quality time with their teenagers. The lack of attention from parents can cause children to turn to their own friends for their values, acceptance, and self-esteem. In the functional family, the parents are the first line of defense for the children against negative peer pressure. Recognizing the need for open communication with their children, the parents do not expect the local church, youth group, or high school to take on this primary responsibility. An effective church youth group can be tremendous support for teens during their formative years, but it does not take the place of parents in a functional system.

Helpers working with families affected by a member's life-controlling problem should encourage parents to stand together in guarding against coalitions. When a single parent makes a decision to stand firm or a husband and wife stand together in helping their son or daughter, it is not uncommon for the child to try to start a coalition with a grandparent or a friend close to the family.

The helper should remember that each person is not an island. Each person is a part of a family system. Although dysfunctional patterns may have developed over a period of years, helpers can encourage family members to restore proper relationships.

A Final Thought

You may have read this chapter and thought about all the wrong things you have done in your family life. Maybe some are in a marriage where one partner wants to follow God's plan for the marriage and the family wholeheartedly while the other partner prefers to do his or her "own thing." Whether you read this chapter while considering following Christ as Savior, having just recently received Christ as Savior, or having been a Christian for several years, you may now have an important question on your mind. "My family is in a mess; I've been a poor parent. My kids are messed up on drugs, and I am in my third marriage. My third spouse is about to leave me, and my youngest son is going to prison. What should I do?"

In 2 Samuel 24, David sinned greatly against the Lord by his disobedience. God instructed Gad to "Go and tell David, 'This is what the LORD says: I am giving you three options. Choose one of them for me to carry out against you' "(v11). None of the options were good.

David gave Gad his decision. "I am in deep distress. Let us fall into the hands of the LORD, for his mercy is great; but do not let me fall in the hands of men" (v14). Although God held David responsible for his actions, David preferred to "fall in the hands of the LORD."

Then what shall we do with our failed marriage and family relationships? First, fall into the hands of God. Second, do all you can to follow God's principles in all your marriage and family relationships. And finally, leave the consequences to God.

8

$\mathscr{H}$and-Me-Downs

Family members often hand down inspirational and valuable items to their children—antiques, rings, the family Bible, and property. My wife's grandmother lived nearly 104 years. She did not have many earthly possessions, but her godly life-style has been handed down to family members. In her family are ministers, medical and business professionals, and church and community leaders. Grandma's hand-me-downs, though not silver and gold, are an asset to society.

Other hand-me-downs can result in pain, dysfunction, and aimlessness. A child sits in a restaurant with his parents and observes them drinking alcohol. Unknowingly, they may be training the child to take the first step that could lead to addiction.

A husband shows no respect for his wife and, by example, teaches this behavior to his son. His son will likely show a lack of respect for his wife. Abusive parents are often the products of abuse or neglect themselves.

Immediately after Max concluded his presentation on "Family Dependencies" to a high school faculty, a teacher approached him with tears in her eyes. Margaret, a math teacher, explained that she was a divorcee of three months. Her former husband was controlled by alcohol and compulsive spending. She explained how she was physically and emotionally abused during this ten-year marriage. The couple was in debt to the point of having to declare bankruptcy. Concerned about her children because they were being neglected, she chose a painful divorce to alleviate this family tension.

As the conversation continued, Margaret explained that her father was an alcoholic. As a child, she had given much of her time serving as the mom of the family since most of her mother's energy and efforts were given to her alcoholic husband. Margaret would sometimes help the younger children prepare for school and cook their meals when her mother was not available to care for them. In this lengthy conversation, Margaret finally got to the point. "Max, you have given a description of my family. With all the pain and suffering I have experienced with my former husband and father, I can't believe what I am doing. I have started a relationship with a nice man who accepts me, and we are making plans for marriage. Here's the problem! I believe he is also an alcoholic. How could I do this again to my children and myself?"

Whenever a family member has a life-controlling problem, the entire family is affected. These strongholds can be handed down from generation to generation if the chain of sin is not broken. Moses writes: "'The LORD is slow to anger, abounding in love and forgiving sin and rebellion. Yet he does not leave the guilty unpunished; he punishes the children for the sin of the fathers to the third and fourth generation'" (Numbers 14:18). "Church and community are concerned with the stability of family life. Family instability contributes inordinately to human suffering 'unto the third and fourth generation'" (Turnbull, 221).

Various theories explain why dependencies run in families. Some experts believe it is hereditary; others contribute it to a person's environment. Frank Minirth, a noted psychiatrist, has said:

> Alcoholism runs in families, but it is not clear whether this pattern
> relates more to hereditary or environmental influence. If an "addic-

tion-prone" trait is passed genetically, the specific trait has not been identified. . . .

There is reason to believe that there may be some genetic difference in many but not all alcoholics. But genetics is not the only reason individuals become alcoholics. Nor does every person with this genetic difference become an alcoholic (60-61).

Although much attention is given to alcoholism running in families, this is also true of other dependencies. The children of compulsive gamblers learn behaviors that are transferred to the next generation. They have many of the same symptoms that are seen in drug addictions. Child abuse is another problem that runs in families. "*Abusive parents* frequently were themselves abused or neglected in childhood" (Collins, 455, 1980).

Codependency

Mildred walked into her minister's office one morning and informed him she was divorcing her husband, Al. The minister had noticed that she had become indifferent toward the church, but he did not know why. She actually had much to be thankful for because Al received Christ as his Savior 13 months ago. After experiencing a dramatic conversion, he also had a remarkable recovery from alcoholism.

Prior to Al's conversion, Mildred had regularly asked for prayer for him and often told of her struggles of trying to care for him. She impressed the church with her persistence. Enduring this horrible tragedy of life, she was seen by some as a saint. Pastor Hudson had noticed on several occasions in her comments that she seemed to take pride in her suffering.

Mildred took pride in caring for Al's addiction. Her sense of well-being came from being his caretaker. When Al was converted and became sober, her purpose for living seemed to end. His addiction gave her the sense of well-being she needed. Her life was focused on Al versus Christ for her self-esteem. Mildred was codependent. Shortly after the divorce, Mildred met another alcoholic and later married him. In her quest for self-esteem, she continued the codependent behaviors with her new husband.

Codependency is a popular word used to describe people's behavior when they are addicted to another person. Although this word may be faddish, I do not know of a better term to use. This term surfaced in the late seventies; however, the behaviors were in existence long before then. Melody Beattie defines a codependent person as "one who has let another person's behavior affect him or her, and who is obsessed with controlling that person's behavior" (31).

Codependency involves those who take ownership of another person's problem, get a sense of well-being from that person, or allow themselves to be controlled by that person's dependent behaviors. That person's master becomes the friend or relative instead of God. Paul writes in his letter to the Romans: "They exchanged the truth of God for a lie, and worshiped and served created things rather than the Creator" (1:25).

Codependent Relationships

There are certain characteristics that develop in codependent relationships. According to Kathy Capell-Sowder, a person who has a love relationship with an addicted person will demonstrate certain symptoms: increase in tolerance, denial, compromise in value system, major-life areas decline, trapped in the victim's role, plans to escape, addictions develop in other areas (Capell-Sowder, 20-23).

Increase in tolerance. The excuses from the dependent person are increasingly accepted. The codependent individual experiences an increased loss of control over feelings, mood swings, acceptance of blame, and responses to the addicted person. There is a decline in his or her self-worth along with increased feelings of inadequacy. A wall of defenses designed to help the codependent and other family survive in the relationship to the dependent loved one is built.

Denial. Feeling the need to protect and cover up for the behavior of the dependent person, the co-addict joins the loved one in denial. Ignoring the problem and thinking things will get better when they are getting worse contribute to the numbing process of feelings. Codependent individuals deny their lifestyles are affected by a spouse's stronghold. They may deny their own needs because of their concern for the children. Losing touch with reality, they continue in denial resulting in distorted thinking which leads to a state of delusion.

Compromise in value system. Codependents give much time caring for dependent spouses. Their lack of self-worth may cause problems. They may fall prey to an affair that is totally opposite their values. Their excessive attention given to a spouse may cause the children to be neglected or even abused. Having been raised in church, they may even abandon their commitment to spiritual matters. Betrayal of their value system will increase guilt causing them to feel unsure about their personal identity.

Major life areas decline. As the addiction process affects the dependent's emotional, spiritual, and physical well-being, so it is with the codependent. In the co-addicted role, a person's emotions are affected by the strain on the marriage. Co-addicted persons begin to doubt themselves and feel the pain over a spouse lost to a life-controlling problem. They may neglect their responsibilities to the children or even abuse them.

Codependents may begin to feel that God does not love them or that they have disappointed God, and there may be feelings of isolation from the Lord. They may experience physical problems including chronic headaches and backaches that are stress related. Employers may notice frequent absences and hospital visits.

Trapped in the victim's role. The impaired thinking of codependents now has them confused without the ability to see their options. They feel trapped because they have lost control of their lives. They do not know how to take options that may be before them because they are in a state of delusion. Co-addictive behaviors have led to an unmanageable life. Feeling trapped, they may sense hopelessness and begin to look for a way to escape from the relationship.

Plans to escape. Codependents may escape by separating or divorcing the spouse. Plans may include having a suitcase packed for departure at all times. They may save money and wait for the children to finish school, then feel free to exit the relationship. Even if they do leave, it may be for only a short period of time, or they may start another relationship with a compulsive person. The co-addictive attachment seems to bring them back to the dysfunctional relationship. They may eventually lose all hope and consider suicide as their way of escape.

Addictions in other areas. Codependents may develop addictions in other areas including gambling, compulsive eating, religion, compulsive spending, or working. Even if codependents exit the relationship with the addicted loved one, they may start another addictive relationship. Codependents become trapped in an addictive system, and it is difficult to break free.

The first step begins with helping codependents break out of their own delusions through awareness. "Overcoming addiction is as much building positive involvements in one's environment as it is withdrawing from addictive attachments" (Capell-Sowder, 22-23). Abstinence or freedom from the life-controlling problem is not enough. A whole new relationship has to be built.

Codependency and Christian Balance

The subject of codependency should be approached with balance. According to Paul, the body of Christ should be interdependent (*see* Romans 12:7-16; 1 Corinthians 12:12-27). Codependency, however, is unhealthy because the person is mastered by a loved one's problem or has become a loved one's master (playing God).

It is possible to live an unbalanced life regarding codependency. On one hand, a person may be totally dependent on a friend or loved one for a sense of well-being. On the other hand, an individual may become self-centered in his or her lifestyle without regard for a friend or loved one.

Codependents need to be encouraged to focus on a Christ-centered life versus being addicted to the friend or loved one. The writer of Hebrews says, "Let us fix our eyes on Jesus, the author and perfecter of our faith, who for the joy set before him endured the cross, scorning its shame, and sat down at the right hand of the throne of God" (12:2). Codependents should be encouraged to turn their dependency toward God rather than to the dependent friend or loved one.

How to Help a Codependent Person

Helping a codependent move from unhealthy to healthy relationships is a process. Since the codependent is suffering from impaired thinking much like the dependent person, the helper needs to exhibit trustworthiness. Codependents have a low level of trust and need role models who are honest and stable. To be effective, the helper needs to display realistic honesty yet offer hope. Codependents need a helper who mirrors truth, helping them acknowledge obsessive and compulsive behaviors toward the dependent loved one.

The helper should expect codependents to be responsible for their actions. Enabling codependents by mopping up after them or being sympathetic to their self-pity does not help. Codependents need encouragement interacted with accountability. The helper should encourage codependents to be involved in a Christian support group that provides concern, love, and accountability because they need assistance in understanding the three *C*s. First, they need to understand that they did not *cause* their loved one's problem. Many times codependents blame themselves for their loved one's addiction. Feeling they are responsible for the dependent's behavior greatly contributes to codependents' low self-worth. The helper should help codependents understand that their loved one is responsible for the choices that have led to addiction no matter what the circumstances may be.

Second, codependents need to understand they cannot *control* their loved one's dependency. It is common for codependents to feel a need to control the loved one's problem by covering up for them or keeping them out of trouble. Trying to control them through manipulation, domination, and guilt only leads to a greater loss of energy. Helpers should assist codependents in understanding that they cannot fix their loved one; instead, they should let go of trying to *play God*. Accepting this fact of powerlessness over the loved one is the first step of recovery for the codependent.

Third, codependents need to understand they cannot *cure* their loved one. The anger and hurt intensify as codependents see their inability to cure their loved one through caretaking. Helpers should encourage codependents to cast anxiety on the Lord (*see* 1 Peter 5:7). Codependents need to understand they are not responsible for their loved one's cure. Since their focus has been clouded by their loved one's behavior, they will probably need assistance in directing their focus toward Christ. Unknowingly, their lives have likely become centered around their loved ones to the point of serving them above God. The man of God warned Eli in 1 Samuel 2:29 about this very concern: "Why do you honor your sons more than me?"

Helpers should assist codependents in understanding the importance of focusing on Christ. Their self-identity and freedom come from being *in Christ*. Codependents need to turn loose of their own identity and take on their God-given identity *in Christ*. Jesus says in Matthew 16:24-25: "If anyone would come after me, he must deny himself and take up his cross and follow me. For whoever wants to save his life will lose it, but whoever loses his life for me will find it."

Codependents' personal downgrading thoughts of themselves can be transformed into new identity by understanding that their significance comes from being in Christ. Also with this identity, freedom and confidence can be gained. "In him and through faith in him we may approach God with freedom and confidence" (Ephesians 3:12). As it is with all other human needs, establishing a personal relationship with Jesus Christ is the most effective way in overcoming codependent relationships. "Whoever comes to me I will never drive away" (John 6:37).

Children of Dependent Parents

After concluding his sermon on Sunday morning as guest minister, Max was greeted by a young man. With tears flowing down his cheeks, eighteen-year-old Mike presented Max with a tough question: "What is a normal family?"

He explained to Max that both of his parents were alcoholics. He went on to say that he was converted to Christ one year ago. He had made plans to enter seminary with the assistance of his extended family, his church. Having been raised as a child of dependent parents, Mike had no idea what a normal family life was like. His church loved him enough to show him God's love, but he still struggled with painful memories.

Forty-year-old Raymond explained to Jim that he had a good marriage. His family was active in church, and he was a successful businessman. He explained that he was thankful for his family because he could not remember ever being a child. His parents sexually abused him and were also alcoholics. Raymond said, "Although I have a good family, I still mourn because I did not have a childhood." Then he asked Jim a difficult question: "How long must I mourn?" Although Jim did not have the answer, he did suggest that Raymond allow God to turn his mourning into compassion for other children of dependent parents.

Various Stages

Children of dependent parents go through similar stages. Although there has been much written on children of alcoholics, the children of gamblers, sexaholics, even workaholics face similar problems. When a parent is in bondage to a life-controlling problem, there is instability in the home. Gary Collins in his work on Christian counseling states:

> When parents are not getting along with each other, children feel anxious, guilty and angry. They are anxious because the stability of

the home is threatened, guilty because they are afraid that they may have caused the strife, and angry because they often feel left out, forgotten, and sometimes manipulated into taking sides—which they do not want to do. Sometimes there also is a fear of being abandoned. Unstable homes, therefore, often (but not always) produce unstable children (206, 1980).

Learned behavior. Living with difficult situations, these children learn to cope with stress. They learn how to protect themselves from possible harm. They learn not to talk about the problem. The addicted parent is like a big, white elephant in the living room. Everybody sees him, but nobody talks about him. Being raised in an unstable home causes children to lose trust. They learn to suppress their feelings. Oftentimes, they become nonfeeling individuals.

Seeking out behavior. During this time of searching, a caring person may see hints of a problem in these children. They will usually exhibit characteristics of being a perfect, rebellious, withdrawn, or funny child. In this stage they may attempt to control their parent's dependency. Delusion sets in and enabling behaviors start in this stage.

Harmful behavior. The children's compulsiveness will display a forceful defense in this stage. They feel locked in without strength to make choices. Their behavior becomes a role to deny pain and to cope. They feel responsible for their parent's dependency and blame themselves. "As we have seen, it is a normal part of the development process for children to feel that they are the center of the universe and consequently responsible for the good and the bad things that happen to their friends, siblings and parents" (O'Gorman, 112). Their painful lifestyle becomes normal.

Escape. Children of dependent parents may act on negative feelings. Escape from the painful lifestyle often results in separation, desertion, or even suicide. As these children approach adulthood, they are likely to carry their defensive lifestyle with them to the next relationship. Unhealthy relationships are common among the adult children of dependent parents.

Feelings

Children of dependent parents learn to repress their feelings. To prevent *rocking the boat,* they restrain their emotions. Anger builds as the children move back and forth between a love and hate relationship with their parents. Feeling responsible for their parents, they blame themselves. This self-blame internalizes, bringing on painful emotions. These children may have low self-worth with shameful feelings.

Their feelings are affected by a life of isolation and loneliness. These children live with the fear of being abandoned by their parents at any moment. They fear the unexpected since their parents' behavior is so unpredictable. For example, the father tells his son he will take him fishing on Saturday. He breaks his promise because he is *hung over* from his alcohol consumption on Friday night. When they receive very little attention, these neglected children experience painful emotions. They feel mixed-up, confused, and boxed-in since they are trapped without options that may free them.

Survival Behaviors

Children condition themselves to cover their pain. Concerned about getting their needs met, they may give in to behaviors that betray their values. The oldest child in the family may take on the role of the mother or father in being responsible for the other children. "I've seen five-year-olds running entire families," says Janet Geringer Woititz (Leerhsen and Namuth, 63). These children are known to be loyal to their parents even when loyalty is harmful or undeserved. To protect themselves from physical harm during a parent's drunken condition, some children have been known to sleep with large knives or hammers under their pillows.

Having a need to survive, these children develop certain roles. Usually the *perfect child* takes on the responsibility of the other children. This is often the oldest child. This child is likely to excel in academics, sports, or other school activities and usually becomes a leader in adulthood. Having an unhealthy desire to be perfect, this child needs help in understanding his or her feelings.

The *rebellious child* acts out negative feelings and frustrations. In an attempt to get attention, this child will probably resort to antisocial behavior. The child may turn to drugs as a means of escape. Such a child needs boundaries and should be made responsible for personal actions. It is common for other family members to take out their frustrations on this child.

The *withdrawn child,* often the middle child, suffers from poor self-esteem. This child is usually a loner with limited self-expectations and has difficulty building friendships. Not knowing where he or she fits in, this child may have difficulty with personal identity. Since there has been parental role inconsistencies, this child needs help in overcoming fear. Helpers should assist the victim in recognizing personal strengths.

The *clown* is usually the youngest child who has been overprotected by other family members. The child is likely to be immature. Although intelligent, he or she may have difficulty in concentrating. This child needs help in accepting responsibility. Getting caught up in the child's silly behavior is not helpful; rather, accountability and meaningful self-direction is needed. Understanding these roles as defense systems is important for the helper. Charles Leerhsen and Tessa Namuth further report:

> A high achiever in school, the Hero always does what's right, often discounting himself by putting others first. The Lost Child, meanwhile, is withdrawn, a loner on his way to a jobless adulthood, and thus, in some ways, very different from the Scapegoat, who appears hostile and defiant but inside feels hurt and angry. . . . Last and least—in his own mind—is the Mascot, fragile and immature yet charming: the family clown (67).

Although much has been written concerning children of alcoholics and the roles they play, these roles also exist in most families.

However, in dysfunctional systems, they are more noticeable since they become coping devices.

Without Help

Without help, the children of dependent parents may have a trail of problems. Feeling responsible for everything, they may become workaholics or develop other compulsive behaviors. They are likely to show little zest for life. Having a lack of trust, they have difficulty in building meaningful relationships. Their potential may never be discovered.

They are likely to marry a dependent person, starting the merry-go-round of problems again. Having no guidelines for parenting, adult children of dependent parents often resort to the way they were raised. Normal behavior for a functional family is unknown to them. They often make decisions without consideration for the consequences. Judging themselves harshly becomes standard practice.

With Help

With assistance, children of dependent parents can develop functional relationships. Having self-discipline, they can become good leaders, dependable, and responsible. They learn to accept responsibility with an understanding of reality. Some of the best role models and creative people are children of dependent parents who have received help. They are normally willing to help others. Although many of the children have lived in horrible conditions, they can learn to let go and have fun.

A Biblical Perspective

Moses writes in Exodus 20:5-6, "For I, the LORD your God, am a jealous God, punishing the children for the sin of the fathers to the third and fourth generation of those who hate me, but showing love to a thousand generations of those who love me and keep my commandments." Much is said about children being under the curse of their parents' sin. Children are not responsible for their parents' sin. There are scriptures that clearly support this fact. "Fathers shall not be put to death for their children, nor children put to death for their fathers; each is to die for his own sin" (Deuteronomy 24:16). "The soul who sins is the one who will die. The son will not share the guilt of the father, nor will the father share the guilt of the son" (Ezekiel 18:20).

Notice again in Exodus 20:6, "but showing love to a thousand generations of those who love me and keep my commandments." Our focus should be on this part of the so called "generational curse" in these verses. In a court case it was stated, "There are no illegitimate children, only illegitimate parents." Children often grow up to be dysfunctional in their lifestyles when their parents were that type of role model. "If we, as parents, live sinful and psychologically unhealthy lives, there will be a profound effect upon our children, grandchildren, and perhaps other descendants as well. God is not punishing our offspring for our sins, *we are*, by not living the right way" (Meier, Ratcliff, and Rowe, 45).

In 2 Chronicles 33-35, there is a narrative of hand-me-down behaviors and a stop to this trap. Josiah was raised in what is called today a dysfunctional family. His grandfather, Manasseh, was a very wicked king. His influence harmed many people. "But Manasseh led Judah and the people of Jerusalem astray, so that they did more evil than the nations the LORD had destroyed before the Israelites" (33:9).

Amon was Josiah's father. Amon continued in his father's ways. "He did evil in the eyes of the LORD, as his father Manasseh had done. Amon worshiped and offered sacrifices to all the idols Mannasseh had made" (33:22). He was assassinated by his own officials, and Josiah became king at the age of eight.

Josiah did not follow the example that had been established by his father and grandfather but chose another direction for his life. He focused on "what was right in the eyes of the LORD and walked in the ways of his father David, not turning aside to the right or to the left" (34:2). He focused on the future instead of wallowing in the past.

While he was still young, Josiah went directly to God for direction. "In the eighth year of his reign, while he was still young, he began to seek the God of his father David" (34:3). He put action to his prayers by purging Judah and Jerusalem of false gods. He had the Baal alters destroyed and smashed the Asherah poles and idols. Instead of feeling sorry for himself and blaming his state of condition on the lack of funding by the Judean government, he assumed responsibility as evidenced by his action.

As in any society, when Josiah sought God and became responsible, his heart was drawn to the temple of God. The temple had been neglected, so he gave instructions to have it repaired. Money was given, and the workers were organized and worked faithfully. As they were working one day, "Hilkiah said to Shaphan the secretary, 'I have found the Book of the Law in the temple of the LORD' " (34:15). When Josiah received the book from Shaphan, he repented and saw that his father had not kept the word of the LORD and had "not acted in accordance with all that is written in this book" (34:21). He immediately placed a priority on God's Word as the sole authority and proclaimed it to the people both small and great.

> He read in their hearing all the words of the Book of the Covenant, which had been found in the temple of the LORD. The king stood by his pillar and renewed the covenant in the presence of the LORD—to follow the LORD and keep his commands, regulations and decrees with all his heart and all his soul, and to obey the words of the covenant written in the book (34:30-31).

The chain of hand-me-downs was broken in Josiah's life. His influence brought about a turn in the lives of the people throughout his entire life. "As long as he lived, they did not fail to follow the LORD, the God of their fathers" (34:33).

Hand-me-downs are also discussed in the New Testament. "Many have undertaken to draw up an account of the things that have been fulfilled among us, just as they were handed down to us by those who from the first were eyewitnesses and servants of the word" (Luke 1:1-2). God's Word and influence can be handed down to the next generation. However, unhealthy paradigms can be handed down also. Peter described them as "the empty way of life handed down to you from your forefathers" (1 Peter 1:18). Futile behavior patterns, traditions, and lifestyles are often handed down from generation to generation.

There is hope for sons and daughters who have been handed down dysfunctional pain. First, God is fair. Our Father "judges each man's work impartially" (1 Peter 1:17). Children reared by an abusive or neglectful father often have an incorrect view of God, picturing Him as their earthly father. The good news is our Heavenly Father is perfect and fair.

However, God's impartiality does not take away our personal responsibility. Although we may be influenced by genetic inheritance and social surroundings, this does not negate our personal responsibility to God. We can choose life or death, good or evil.

When one chooses futile behaviors, he or she can be led into enslavement. Paul asked, "Don't you know that when you offer yourselves to someone to obey him as slaves, you are slaves to the one whom you obey—whether you are slaves to sin, which leads to death, or to obedience, which leads to righteousness?" (Romans 6:16). In his book, *Daniel Speaks Today*, Myer Pearlman said concerning sin, "A man is free to begin, but is not always free to quit" (54).

Second, Christ offers release from enslaving hand-me-downs. This comes "not with perishable things such as silver or gold . . . but with the precious blood of Christ, a lamb without blemish or defect" (1 Peter 1:18-19). Christ paid the payment of this release with His precious blood. Jesus said, "So if the Son sets you free, you will be free indeed" (John 8:36).

Third, Jesus knows each of us personally. Before the world began, God had a plan for your release from hand-me-downs. "He was chosen before the creation of the world, but was revealed in these last time for your sake" (1 Peter 1:20). You are more than a number on a computer screen or just another name in a counselor's appointment book. Jesus knows who you are, and He knows your family tree.

Fourth, God will help you walk in His behavior patterns. "Now that you have purified yourselves by obeying the truth so that you have sincere love for your brothers, love one another deeply, from the heart" (1 Peter 1:22). As we believe and obey God's truth, a cleansing power will help us develop godly behavior patterns.

It is interesting to trace our family tree and even do generational behavior studies; however, freedom comes first by being "born again, not of perishable seed, but of imperishable, through the living and enduring word of God" (1 Peter 1:23). To live a life free from enslaving hand-me-downs, it is imperative to walk out God's behavior patterns.

A person who receives Christ as Savior should immediately start a discipleship program to deal with hand-me-downs. Some people who have been saved for years still carry the baggage of hand-me-downs. They also need discipleship. God has boundaries that, when observed, bring His love and blessings. "Stay always within the boundaries where God's love can reach and bless you" (Jude 21, TLB).

Christ-centered support groups which provide both support and accountability can help people who struggle with hand-me-downs. The focus should be on Christ, and the curriculum should emphasize biblical principles of behavior. Confession has its place, but without faith in Christ, one will walk away empty. Paul said, "They must turn to God in repentance and have faith in our Lord Jesus" (Acts 20:21).

The grip of dysfunctional hand-me-downs can be broken. "The grass withers and the flowers fall, but the word of the Lord stands forever" (1 Peter 1:24-25).

Hand-Me-Down Baggage

Many children grow into adulthood carrying baggage they picked up during childhood. Dysfunctional behaviors and belief systems which they learned from their parents are often carried into their adult relationships.

Father vacuum. One of the roles the father plays in the home, whether he knows it or not, is that of modeling our heavenly Father. Many children have grown into adulthood with a distorted view of God our Father because they could not trust their earthly father. When you say "father" to some children, they think of a father who may have been abusive, neglectful, or not there when they needed him. Robert S. McGee in his work, *Father Hunger*, states, "When the average person in the pew thinks in terms of a father who was unexpressive, absent, workaholic, alcoholic, or even, abusive, what is he or she likely to think of God as a heavenly Father?" (19).

Of course, no father can compare with our heavenly Father because no earthly father is perfect. A study of the names of God is a good place to begin for the person who is suffering from a father vacuum or for the man who wants to be a better father. The heavenly Father is the model for the earthly father as provider, healer of hurts, and example of righteousness. Children should see holy living in action through their father. The father should carry the banner of God's love, be the shepherd of the family, and be a presence of peace. One of the names of God that brings assurance and should be practiced by all fathers is being present—*Jehovah-shammah* "THE LORD IS THERE" (Ezekiel 48:35). Those who have a father vacuum can be assured that "God is our refuge and strength, an ever-present help in trouble" (Psalm 46:1).

Guilt-Ridden Parents

One of the most difficult issues for a parent to work through is realizing late in the parenting process that he or she has been a failure as a parent. A father who was helping me one day at our home said, "My son has run away from home and has been gone over a year. We continue to check with the police, but they have no clue as to his whereabouts." Then he said with a broken voice, "I have been a terrible role model. I am now serving the Lord; however, during my son's important years, I was not there for him. My home was the bars."

People who have tremendous guilt due to feelings of failure as a parent often give into inappropriate behavior by their children. A mother who had a 21-year-old son living in her home told my wife and me that sometimes she permitted her son to abuse her verbally and physically. He was also allowed to drink alcohol in the home, and this was against her values. I asked her why she permitted her son to abuse her and drink in her home, and she said, "He had a difficult time during my divorce, and I don't want to hurt him anymore!"

This mother had not been the best of mothers as I later learned. She had committed her life to Christ and was now involved in ministry; however, her past haunted her, and she felt guilty as a parent and would not uphold her newly established value system. It was apparent that the son had lost respect for his mother.

How should this mother respond to her son? I encouraged her to do four things: (1) Have a talk with her son and apologize for her past mistakes as a mother, (2) tell him she loves him too much to permit him to continue his disrespectful attitude and unconcern for her standards in the home, (3) tell him she will always love and pray for him, and (4) tell him she is going to hold him responsible for his actions as God holds her responsible. Along with this information, I encouraged her to be consistent and do all she could to keep the lines of communication open even if he left home.

Some mothers prepare their teenage daughters for premarital sexual activities by helping them with birth control plans. They may feel guilty asking their teenage daughter to abstain from sex outside of marriage especially if they did not. By their own drinking habits, some fathers prepare their sons for their first drink; or by making sexually explicit materials available, they prepare them for premarital sexual encounters. Whether working from guilt or not, this line of thinking contributes to an addictive society. Just because parents have broken the rules does not mean that children must follow in the same pattern. Stand firm, holding them accountable for their actions as long as you are supporting them whether they are living in your home, in a dorm room, or in an apartment.

Fifty-Year-Old Boys

An addictive society is the perfect environment for a life of irre-sponsibility (all play and very little work). Add to this environment many people who have come from a home where there were irre-sponsible or absent parents, and you find many who choose to pur-sue pleasure as their chief goal instead of facing the challenge of life. The consequences of such pleasure seeking are 50-year-old males who are still boys. Michael Horton in his work, *The Law of Perfect Freedom*, explains the mind-set that is centered on self. "In our self-centered, individualistic, now-oriented culture, we can leave our debts from the past in a nursing home and our debts for the future to our children. But for now, it's Miller Time" (134).

While traveling on a busy freeway in Los Angeles, I heard a preacher on the radio describe the difference between a man and a boy. "Boys play house—men build homes. Boys make babies—men raise families. Boys demand their rights—men assume respon-sibility. Boys look for ways to get out of work—men look for work." The Apostle Paul says, "When I was a child, I talked like a child, I thought like a child, I reasoned like a child. When I became a man, I put childless ways behind me" (1 Corinthians 13:11).

The breakdown of the family and its effect on young men have become a social sore that is festering. Over 30 years ago, United States Senator Daniel Patrick Moynihan, who was then the Assistant Secretary of Labor, discussed this issue.

> From the wild Irish slums of the 19th century Eastern seaboard to the riot-torn suburbs of Los Angeles, there is one unmistakable les-son in American history: A community that allows a large number of young men to grow up in broken families, dominated by women, never acquiring any stable relationship to male authority, never acquiring any rational expectations about the future—that com-munity asks for and gets chaos . . . [In such a society] crime, vio-lence, unrest, unrestrained lashing out at the whole social struc-ture—these are not only to be expected, they are very nearly inevitable (Bennett, 53).

If you are dealing with hand-me-down baggage, please go back to the story of Josiah found in 2 Chronicles 33-35 and prayerfully study this passage. Also, look again at the 1 Peter 1:17-25 and focus on this passage. Ask the Lord to help you start a new model of living that will glorify Him.

Ways to Help Family Members

Living in a state of delusion, children of dependent parents have a difficult time seeing reality. Inviting them to share their concerns helps build a trust relationship between the child and the helper. The helper should be a mirror of reality for the victim while modeling honesty. Since the child's needs may have been neglected, the helper should be an active listener. Separating the person from behavior should be practiced by the helper. As with the codependent, the victim should be shown that the child did not cause the parents' problem, the child cannot control it, nor can the child cure it. It is important for the helper to remember that children (and adults) from families with dependencies learn: *don't talk, don't trust, don't feel.*

The church can play a key role in helping families with dependencies. Each family member needs help in developing a healthy relationship. Although a family member may have a dramatic conversion, the addict and the other family members still need support. Having support groups that meet regularly can benefit these people. They can be comforted and learn to comfort others who have similar needs. Paul writes to the church at Corinth: "On him we have set our hope that he will continue to deliver us, as you help us by your prayers" (2 Corinthians 1:10-11).

9

$\mathcal{H}$ow the Church Is Affected

It was on a frigid February Sunday morning in North Pole, Alaska, with the temperature forty degrees below zero Fahrenheit when I heard some of the most devastating news of my life. Little did I know as I rushed from my room to a friend waiting on me in his car to take me to speak at a church that I was about to hear news that would shock the Church worldwide. My friend told me about a prominent evangelist who had just confessed to sexual immorality. I could not believe what I had heard.

I knew of many people who had been led to the Lord through this person's ministry and often marveled at the way God was using him. While many were saddened, the news media did its thing; and some of the more pious said, "I told you this would happen—he got too big for his britches."

While teaching on the east coast, I noticed a well-known church leader's wife in my seminar. I was also aware that her husband had left her for his secretary. At a break she came up to me, not knowing I knew who she was, and said, "You have just described my husband and pornography over a period of six to seven years. Two years ago, he left me and ran off with his secretary. During his journey with pornography, I protected him, not wanting to hurt his ministry. I thought if I prayed and just kept it to myself, things would eventually change. They did. He's gone, and I am a 55-year-old woman with no job skills."

Actually, these types of examples are only the tip of the iceberg. People sitting in the church pew are being influenced by this addictive society. In Chapter 3 we discussed three prominent tools used by Satan: delusion, isolation, and secrecy. Add to this the breakdown of the family, and we see the challenges the Church is now facing.

Jerry Falwell, speaking at a morning service December 2, 1979, said:

> It is my conviction that the family is God's basic unit in society. God's most important unit in society. No wonder then . . . we are in a holy war for the survival of the family. Before a nation collapses, the families of that nation must go down first. What is a local church? Nothing but a congregation of families (Garruth and Ehrlich, 227).

There is no greater evidence of the breakdown of the family than in the church. Pastors are faced with family situations not even heard of 20 years ago. I believe that we in the Church as a whole are hiding behind our Sunday smiles.

The Mind-Set in the Pew

Although there are numerous exceptions to this mind-set, there is a common thread that seems to run through many evangelical churches of the way people view life as they sit in the pews. It does not matter if it is Baptist, Presbyterian, Nazarene, or Pentecostal, there is a mind-set that comes directly from this addictive society. It is regretful to say, but we have followed the world's pattern of individualism. Chuck Colson describes in his book, *The Body*, his bewilderment by a paradox presented by Gallup, "religion up, morality down." Could it be because of a lack of understanding of God and discipleship? We can be dedicated Christians, be faithful to our churches in support and attendance, and still be influenced by individualism.

> Even Christians who understand their personal identity as followers of Christ will not make a widespread difference in the decline and decay around us—unless we have a high view of our corporate identity as the body of Christ. Many Christians have been infected with the most virulent virus of modern American life, what sociologist Robert Bellah calls "radical individualism." They concentrate on personal obedience to Christ as if all that matters is "Jesus and me," but in so doing miss the point altogether (32).

Individualism is manifested in different ways. Some Christians shut themselves up in their own little world. As Colson says, "Jesus and me" is all that matters to many Christians. I certainly do not want to minimize a person's relationship with Jesus Christ, but we must connect with one another to truly be the body of Christ and make a difference in our society. Jesus said, "As I have loved you, so you must love one another. By this all men will know that you are my disciples, if you love one another" (John 13:34-35). Working together in love is the greatest witness to a community.

Individualism can be ascribed to our church smorgasbord mentality. Instead of being loyal to one church, many families go from church to church preferring the preaching at one, the singing at the next one, and the youth ministry of another. These families are very unlikely to develop one another relationships. The disloyalty factor which is the main concern I hear about from pastors is often rooted in selfishness. Since it is "Jesus and me," we can go where we please and when we decide. The concept of one another relationships was highly visible in the New Testament Church. *In Baby Boomer Blues*, Collins and Clinton say the following concerning baby boomers: "They look for churches that will meet their needs, even if this means going to two churches. And if the churches or their pastors change, the baby boomers can leave as easily as they might shift their grocery shopping from one supermarket to another" (15-16).

The mobility of our society has strengthened individualism. George Barna reports, "People's lives are in a constant state of flux. In the past 5 years, more than 1 out of 4 adults has changed churches; nearly 4 out of 10 have changed their address; most people in the labor pool have changed jobs" (105). This kind of movement makes it difficult for people to develop roots in a local body of believers. Many say they chose not to become involved in the church because they will move again in a short period of time. This is particularly difficult for the children in the family because the relationships they start are often interrupted.

Individualism also contributes to isolation. When we develop a struggle in our lives, we often isolate ourselves from others, particularly those who care. Instead of sharing with a friend, we build a wall around ourselves. In doing so, a false sense of control is developed. The pride of individualism can keep a person from getting the help needed. The mind-set of individualism says, "I don't need your help. I can handle this by myself," or some would say, " 'Jesus and me' have this problem under control." This view is clearly not the New Testament community of believers concept—"encourage one another," "forgive one another," "accept one another," "comfort one another," etc.

How important are the one another relationships in the body of believers? Jesus said, "Love the Lord your God with all your heart and with all your soul and with all you mind and with all your strength. . . . Love your neighbor as yourself" (Mark 12:30-31). This statement is a summary of the Ten Commandments (Exodus 20:1-17). The first four commandments deal with our relationship to God—"Love the Lord your God with all your. . . ." The last six commandments focus on our relationship with others—"Love your neighbor as yourself." If we try to love one another in exclusion of the first four commandments which focus on God, we cannot love one another because God is love. Without focus on God, the first commandment, so-called love degenerates merely to nonlasting feelings without absolutes.

In the second part of Jesus' statement in Mark 12:31, He said, "Love your neighbor as yourself." Then how do we love our neighbor as ourselves? We love in action. Love is an attitude which cannot be measured except by behavioral expressions. The Christian life can be summarized by this: It is a relationship with God and others. Yes, God is first, but we cannot reflect His love by living a life of individualism. We reflect Jesus Christ in one another relationships. I will repeat a statement from Chapter 4. You need the people of God. The people of God need you.

Those Kinds of People

Having served a number of years with Teen Challenge, a ministry which provides residential and outreach care for people with life-controlling problems, I have heard this statement numerous times, "Jimmy, I appreciate your working with those kinds of people."

A few years ago I had concluded speaking on a Sunday morning at a church where Teen Challenge students attended. After I spoke, a lady asked the pastor if she could make some comments about Teen Challenge. She stood at the front of the church and directed her thoughts to the 20 or so boys on the front two pews in the left section of the church as if the four or five hundred other people were not there. Her comments were good, but it was as if not a single soul in that church needed help but those boys. I thought to myself, "Lady, these boys acknowledge they need help. They are in a program 24 hours a day trying to get their lives back together. "Her speech was to "those kinds of people."

As I listened to her talk, I could not help but think of the other four or five hundred people in the church. Sitting there were fathers and mothers with children who desperately needed help, a businessman with an alcohol problem that had not yet surfaced, one-third of a teen group that was sexually active, and a mother struggling with masturbation, just to name a few.

We often pin labels on people which segregate them as losers or sick and prevent them and others from reaching out for help because they fear being tagged with a label. Developing a healthy one another community of believers can eliminate a "those kinds of people" mentality. In Chapter 10, we discuss ways to break down the segregation of people in churches, turning "those people" and "our kind of people" into just "us." In 1 Corinthians 6:9-11, the Apostle Paul discusses life-controlling problems such as sexual immorality, adultery, homosexuality, and drunkenness. However, notice that he does not pin each of them with a label. "And that is what some of you were. But you were washed, you were sanctified, you were justified in the name of the Lord Jesus Christ and by the Spirit of our God" (v11). Yes, they had a new label. They were "in Christ." It was not, "Hello, my name is John. I am a sex addict." Instead, it would be more like this, "Hello, my name is John. I am in Christ. I am not where I need to be, but Jesus is still working on me."

Quick Fix

This addictive society has influenced the Church in quick fixes. It is a part of our society. I cannot wait. I must have it now. One-hour oil changes, photo, printing services, etc. Much of the food industry is built on fast-food restaurants. We are busy, so we pick up a hamburger, fries, and a coke at McDonald's and do business or talk to a friend on our mobile phone as we travel in our car.

Many people take this quick fix mind-set into the church. They expect a polished sermon delivered in the time allotted, and God forbid if the preacher goes past 12 noon. Some people do not seem to like overtime in the church nearly as much as watching a football game go into overtime. So pastors and laypeople work hard to do studies to find what will interest people in attending their church. It has gotten to the point where much of the emphasis is on making people feel good whatever it takes; therefore, the religious section of the newspaper rivals the entertainment section.

Many pastors and their staffs are running themselves crazy to keep up with the latest fad just to make people feel good. I do not want to undermine any effort by pastors to draw crowds if it is to lead people to Christ. However, if it is just to keep up with the First Church across town, then we have missed the point badly.

I can understand the dilemma many ministers face. In a quick fix society, people often look for quick fixes for family problems, financial distress, and physical needs. It is easy for ministers to get in a mode of self-performance. I am convinced that false testimonies of healings, financial successes, name-it and claim-it miracles, etc., have been claimed by those who felt compelled to perform lest people think God was not working in their lives. On the other hand, some ministers are facing the same quick fix problems but are trying to address people's needs with church liturgy without the substance of the Holy Spirit's presence and direction. They fear breaking tradition out of fear of being likened to Pentecostals.

In Isaiah 5 and 6, the prophet pronounces several woes. These woes include those who "run after their drinks," "call evil good and good evil," and "are wise in their own eyes." In Isaiah 6:5, the prophet cries, "Woe to me! . . . I am ruined! For I am a man of unclean lips, and I live among a people of unclean lips, and my eyes have seen the King, the LORD Almighty." Isaiah had come to the point after pronouncing these woes that he saw himself in the presence of Almighty God.

There is another woe in this passage that I have read for years but had overlooked. "Woe . . . to those who say, 'Let God hurry, let him hasten his work so we may see it. Let it approach, let the plan of the Holy One of Israel come, so we may know it' " (Isaiah 5:19). We may want God to hurry in dealing with a situation so that we and others can see it. The lesson is we pray but God works in his own timing. Quick answers, slow answers, or no answers, God is still God. God's working is not based on our self-performance, how well the choir sings, or how many are on the Sunday school roll.

Isaiah came to the real issue. All the woes in life cannot compare with "Woe to me! . . . I am ruined! For I am a man of unclean lips, and I live among a people of unclean lips, and my eyes have seen the King, the LORD Almighty." After this Isaiah "heard the voice of the Lord saying, 'Whom shall I send? And who will go for us?' And I said, 'Here am I. Send me!' " (Isaiah 6:8-9). The bottom line in Isaiah's life was the fear of God, not crowds, results, or "make me feel good."

There are no shortcuts to discipleship. I have seen people instantaneously delivered from drugs, alcohol, and other mastering problems; however, if such people are not discipled, they will likely go back to their former lifestyle. There are no quick fixes, and no one is exempt from the process of discipleship. Growth takes time. Avoiding the Christian growth process results in what I call plastic Christians. I have a tree in my office. It is green year round and it looks like a real tree, but it is plastic. It fools a lot of people, but the truth is it has no life and will never grow because it is plastic. Christians in this quick fix society cannot find realness in themselves or with God by being a plastic Christian. People can say all the right things, know the "in" clichés, and be able to name the top contemporary Christian artist; but there is something missing if they are not building into their schedule a relationship with Christ and others. Covey in *The Seven Habits of Highly Effective People* says the following concerning personal growth:

> I have seen the consequences of attempting to shortcut this natural process of growth often in the business world, where executives attempt to "buy" a new culture of improved productivity, quality, morale, and customer service with strong speeches, smile training. . . . But they ignore the low-trust climate produced by such manipulations (38).

Covey's example in the business world is no different than Christian growth. Much of the low trust in Christian circles can be contributed to the lack of personal Christian growth. This development growth cannot be substituted, ignored, or gained by shortcuts. The greatest need in the Church today is not more miracles, impressive buildings, or impressive crowds but for the Christian to walk in communion with God and His Word on a daily basis with an outflow of love to others. Many try to shortcut this development process, and the result is defeated Christians without a reflection of God's grace in their lives.

Restlessness in the Pew

Another characteristic of this addictive society's affecting the Church is restlessness. This fast-paced society has difficulty dealing with time even when it is available. Dr. Archibald D. Hart believes:

> It is actually possible for us to become addicted to our own adrena-
> line. . . . It is especially easy for many of us to get hooked on the
> challenges of a job or career, because attachment to work is so high-
> ly valued in our work-centered culture. While "workaholism" can
> sometimes mask home problems or basic insecurities, most often it
> is an addiction to the adrenaline surges brought on by challenge
> and competition (1991, 68-70).

Being controlled by schedules is surely an issue we will continue
to deal with moving into the third millennium. However, relaxation
is preventive medicine as well as healing.

I believe that restlessness in some cases is rooted in fear. There
seems to be a rush to make the last dollar before the bottom falls
out. Some think, "If I don't make the dollar today, I may not have
an opportunity tomorrow." Jesus tells the story about a rich man
who was restless about not having room to store his crops. So the
rich man said, " 'This is what I'll do. I will tear down my barns and
build bigger ones, and there I will store all my grains and my
goods.' And I'll say to myself, 'You have plenty of good things laid
up for many years. Take life easy; eat, drink and be merry.' But God
said to Him 'You fool! This very night your life will be demanded
from you. Then who will get what you have prepared for yourself?'"
(Luke 12:18-20). The rich man was only interested in himself. He
did not entrust his future to God's hand. Restlessness calls for work
or activity at the exclusion of God.

Restlessness is also seen in those who are rarely pleased with
today and always living for tomorrow. "In the morning you will say,
'If only it were evening!' and in the evening, 'If only it were morning!' " (Deuteronomy 28:67). Some people can never settle down in
one-another relationships in a local body of believers because they
are always looking for the "spiritual greener grass" on the other side
of town. This mind-set can be contributed to a lack of personal
Christian growth. How do we replace restlessness with stability? "But
his delight is in the law of the LORD, and on his law he meditates day

and night. He is like a tree planted by streams of water, which yields its fruit in season and whose leaf does not wither. Whatever he does prospers" (Psalm 1:2-3). In the next chapter we will look at ways to make this paradigm shift.

We have a promise in the Bible that gives us confidence as we move into the third millennium. Jesus said, "I will build my church, and the gates of Hades will not overcome it" (Matthew 16:18).

10

Creating an Environment for Healing and Growth

The Church is made up of all true believers, both Jew and gentile. The Church is an organism in which all believers have a living union in Christ. Local churches which are communities of believers in local assemblies and various localities of single groups comprise the Church. Examples of local churches in the New Testament were "the church of God in Corinth" (1 Corinthians 1:2), "saints in Christ Jesus at Philippi" (Philippians 1:1), and "the church of the Thessalonians" (1 Thessalonians 1:1). "While local churches may develop extensive organizations, the work of God is done primarily through the church as an organism, directed by Christ the Head in keeping with the capacities of each individual member" (Chafer and Walvoord, 277).

Because an addictive society is dysfunctional and perpetual, ministry in this type of society is difficult. We need help in seeing beyond our own paradigms particularly since they are so enforced in our society. A lady recently told me of the bondage in her family that had been there for years. "My husband and I have faithfully served the Lord for many years, but there was something that was not right. It has only been in the last year that I saw my baggage clearly. Through my relationship with Christ and others in a small group, I was set free."

A gentleman from a small midwestern city stated, "This group has been an answer to prayer. I have grown spiritually more in ten weeks through this group than I have in 20 years." A pastor reported the power of Christ-centered, one another relationships in his church.

> I have seen several new decisions for Jesus Christ, real healings in all types of situations, and many marriages brought back together in the name of Jesus. I have found that the best thrill of all is to see God healing marriages which were heading for divorce . . . . To see the whole family in church now all praising God is the beautiful fruits of the active Word of God applied through [our small groups].

Looking at the various aspects of this society—the breakdown of family and community, life-controlling problems, and hand-me-downs—we see they are also having an influence on the Church. A change from patterns of dysfunction to models of healthy and functional relationships is not only the right change, but it is also overdue.

Carl F. George in his book, *The Coming Church Revolution*, talks about the changing church and how to be prepared. He discusses the meta-church which "means a church in transition, a church that is turning, a church that is becoming" (27). He says "people are dropping out of churches because they're not being assimilated into the life (or relationships) of the church" (32). It is time to review our models and patterns of how we "do church." With Christ as our foundation and the Bible our road map, the paradigm shift will require more attention to relationship-based ministry. To go a step further, it must become our model because it was the pattern of the New Testament Church. "They broke bread in their homes and ate together with glad and sincere hearts, praising God and enjoying the favor of all the people" (Acts 2:46-47).

I am thankful for the seminary training I received, but it was inferior to the training in ministry I received from my father. I have learned much from college courses in business administration as it relates to ministry; nevertheless, it does not compare with what I learned through a relationship with the late Hugh O. Maclellan, Sr., who was chairman of the Maclellan Foundation. He taught by example. His emphasis was on building relationships—friendships. His interpretation of fund raising was friend raising.

Many times we tried to honor Mr. Maclellan for his achievements in touching so many people; however, he always preferred to remain behind the scenes and give the credit to the schools, principals, teachers, students, churches, and pastors. I spoke with him every six to seven weeks about ministry projects. His first question was not "How are you doing?" but "How are we doing?" He truly knew what it meant to be God's fellow workers.

My greatest remembrance of Mr. Maclellan goes back to 1981 when we were discussing the start-up of Project 714 and its possible expansion. I discussed with him the many risk factors involved in expanding a school-based drug prevention/intervention program. He looked at me with his usual gentleness and asked this question with firm conviction, "What are the risks if we choose to do nothing?"

As we move into the third millennium, we must focus on a return to our foundations and our relationship with Christ and with others. Most evangelical churches do a good job of emphasizing a personal relationship with Jesus Christ. However, we often lack the needed focus on the community of believers as it relates to our relationship with God.

What are some of the more important "nuts and bolts" of becoming a relationship-based church? We discussed in Chapter 5 the three primary resources used by God, and one of those resources is the people of God. In this chapter we will focus on some of the important aspects of developing the people of God into a relationship-based body of believers.

The Message of the Cross

First, the message of the cross has not changed. Paul states, "I am not ashamed of the gospel, because it is the power of God for the salvation of everyone who believes: first for the Jew, then for the Gentile" (Romans 1:16). The message of the cross need not be compromised to reach people in this society. "God does not alter truth to fit the spirit of the times or the thinking of a contemporary generation. He has not done so in the past; he does not do so today. Methods can be altered but the basic content of the message cannot" (Collins and Clinton, 85).

William Bennett reports in *The Index of Leading Cultural Indicators* that "biblically conservative denominations and other conservative Christian fellowships are among the fastest growing churches" (116). This book of index indicators also shows that some mainline Protestant denominations have lost as many as one-third of their membership since 1965. A first look at these statistics indicates that the gospel of tolerance and compromise is not working. Once the compromise begins, there seems to be no end to the delusion of mankind.

Dealing with the problems in the church at Corinth, Paul emphasized the message of the cross. Dysfunctional relationships and life-controlling problems were common, but Paul chose this message, "For the message of the cross is foolishness to those who are perishing, but to us who are being saved it is the power of God" (1 Corinthians 1:18).

Creating an Environment for Healing and Growth

To create such an environment, we first must picture the church as a mission field. Kennon L. Callahan in *Effective Church Leadership* says, "The day of the professional minister is over. The day of the missionary pastor has come" (3). He further states, "We are called to share the Kingdom, not to grow churches. The fundamental category for this time is mission, not church. What we need is mission growth" (19). Callahan's insight is very important in light of an addictive society. It is easy to get caught up in "greasing the religious wheels" and lose sight of our mission.

For a local church to be effective in helping the hurting, it must provide an environment for healing and growth. This involves love, acceptance, and forgiveness.

An environment of caring and sharing should not be confused with giving a license to sin. Love and acceptance should be addressed in the light of firm love versus sloppy agape. This environment will encourage people to attend a loving church because they feel accepted. Paul describes this love and acceptance: "We loved you so much that we were delighted to share with you not only the gospel of God but our lives as well . . . encouraging, comforting and urging you to live lives worthy of God, who calls you into his kingdom and glory" (1 Thessalonians 2:8,12). A loving and accepting church is one that is winning the right to be heard in its community. This New Testament church will help those who are struggling behind their Sunday smiles.

Utilizing Laypeople

A person does not need to have a Ph.D. to be a people helper. The laity can provide a valuable service in caring for the personal needs of the local church. It is impossible for the ministerial staff to deal with the hurts and staggering needs that most congregations are facing. Actually, this work should be the responsibility of the local body of Christ. This is truly a significant way to release the church to ministry.

Indeed, there would be more laypeople involved in helping those with life-controlling problems, but they feel inadequate. Many churches have been taught that this kind of help should be limited to professionals. L. Rebecca Propst in her work on paraprofessional therapy says:

> Anthony and Carkhuff (1977) define the paraprofessional, or "functional professional" (the term they prefer), as that individual who, lacking formal credentials, performs those functions usually reserved for credentialed mental health professionals . . . various

church workers would also fall in the category. . . . A review of the research in 1968 found that paraprofessionals could be trained to effect significant constructive changes in the clients they worked with (Benner, 88-89).

Although there is very little recent research available regarding their effectiveness, there has been an increase in the number of "functional professionals." I have observed on numerous occasions the effectiveness of laypeople in the areas of encouragement and exhortation. Their effectiveness has not always depended on their degree of education. Those who were most effective exhibited spiritual maturity, emotional stability, knew their limitations, and were blessed with Bible-based common sense.

It is true that some people are drawn to counseling-type ministries because of their own problems. Others may use the helping ministries as a way to build their own egos. "Regrettably, many who are drawn to a counseling role are insecure people intrigued by the opportunity for instant intimacy . . . others find the title 'counselor' personally fulfilling" (Crabb, 163). Caution should be taken to channel enthusiasm into proper directions. Paul provides solid direction in 1 Thessalonians 5:14: "And we urge you, brothers, warn those who are idle, encourage the timid, help the weak, be patient with everyone."

All of us need each other in the community of believers. We need the ministry of each other to help in the development of our walk with God and in understanding the principles of God's Word. The local church is designed to be an interdependent community accountable to the lordship of Jesus Christ. Paul describes the Church in 1 Corinthians 12:12: "The body is a unit, though it is made up of many parts; and though all its parts are many, they form one body."

Helping people with life-controlling problems should be one of the main focuses of lay ministries. It must be remembered that Jesus is the healer (*see* Acts 9:32-35). No minister or layperson can bring healing in the life of a person who is encumbered with a stronghold; however, healing can occur where there is a proper environment of love and acceptance. The ultimate therapist is the Holy

Spirit. A church with laypeople involved in helping ministries can be compared to a garden that has been prepared for the seed to grow. The Lord can use laypeople to clear the wound for the Great Physician to heal the brokenhearted.

"One another" relationships cannot be developed without utilizing laypeople. Dr. Mike Chapman, pastor of Lee Highway Church of God in Chattanooga, Tennessee, says that to view a church flow-chart properly, it should be turned upside down. Carl George says:

> Show me a pastor-centered large church, and we'll find a very tired staff of clergy. Show me a lay-powered, simply organized large church, where the clergy are not completely exhausted because they're doing too much, and I will show you a church that will not stop growing because it will be able to take good care of people as God calls them to new life through it (35).

20-60-20 Ratio

Most churches can be described by what I call the 20-60-20 ratio. Generally speaking, about 20 percent of the people in the local church do most of the work. They are usually the faithful supporters and the ones on whom the pastor can count. Their lives are usually reflected by commitment to God and their church.

The bottom 20 percent are those in the church who are openly struggling with life-controlling issues of substances, behaviors, and/or relationships. Most of the time, people are aware of their struggles. Most recovery-type ministries are geared toward this group of people often ignoring the rest of the congregation as though they do not have problems.

The 60 percent is the group in the middle. This group struggles from time to time, but their problems stay hidden and, at least outwardly, they seem to have their lives together. This part of the church is on a continuum from the top 20 percent to the bottom 20 percent. Many in the bottom 20 percent in the past were a part of the 60 percent.

The Apostle Paul says, "Remember that some men's sins are obvious, and are equally obvious bringing them into judgment. The sins of other men are not apparent, but are dogging them, nevertheless under the surface. Similarly some virtues are plain to see, while others, though not at all conspicuous, will eventually become known" (1 Timothy 5:24-25 PHILIPS). These verses present a picture of the 20-60-20 ratio. In the bottom 20 percent, the "sins are obvious" as the problems are out in the open. Life-controlling problems are directing their lives, "bringing them to judgment," by pointing the way for them.

Some in the top 20 percent and many in the 60 percent have problems that "are not apparent, but are dogging them, nevertheless under the surface." 1 Timothy 5:25 uses the comparison of good deeds to show that those under-the-surface sins "will eventually become known." Although these verses can be interpreted to refer to the sins and good deeds to be revealed when we are judged by God, the principles are applicable now. If destructive behaviors that dog people under the surface are not dealt with, they will become obvious.

Although well-meaning and caring, recovery groups that segregate people with "like problems" can create a "those kinds of people" mentality in the church. People in the top 20 percent or 60 percent are not likely to be a part of a labeled group even though issues which have not surfaced are dogging them. They do not want to be identified with the bottom 20 percent (co-dependents, alcoholics, sex addicts, etc.), so the problems continue to grow. There are some in the top 20 percent who have a child or spouse in the bottom 20 percent but lack an understanding of how to help them and often become a part of the problem.

So, what can we do? We develop relationship-based ministry for the whole church. An approach is discussed in Chapter 13. We develop sermons that show people practical ways to live a free life in Christ. Our Sunday school classes focus on building relationships through God's Word instead of a lecture every week.

We develop small groups that focus on felt needs and friend-to-friend evangelism. The recovery groups that seem to have no goals or end and discuss the same old problems every week should be integrated back into the broader body of believers as soon as possible. When we segregate people by problems, an isolation of understanding is the result. Special needs groups will be necessary, but we will not leave them there to stay. We will help them grow in Christ and move from the "special needs" group to other relationship-based ministry.

Relationship-based ministry in small groups is more than sharing over a cup of coffee. Ministry in an addictive society calls for bonding and friendships that go beyond "plastic" and surface talk. People will know immediately if they are free to share in a group or if they are out of place.

Gary was involved in a church where he felt accepted even though he had a prison record and did not dress according to the latest fashion. This church is a multicultural congregation that spans age, race, and economic problems. Gary says, "I married and after a while ran into some real emotional, financial, and spiritual problems." He also states that he broke his marriage vows and started drinking constantly to escape his problems.

After church discipline, Gary was asked to join a small group. Speaking of his experience in the group, Gary said, "Nobody looked down their nose at me because of my problems, but at the same time nobody in the group condoned my sins. I began to look forward to the meetings."

Later, Gary was transferred by his employer to another city. He found he had difficulty fitting in at his new church because the approach was so different than his former church. Gary explains:

> The home fellowship groups in most churches are good, but they are different from [my former church] groups. If I share some struggles in a home fellowship like I could in [my former group], I feel out of place. In some types of groups, people will not share their problems, and if they share a problem, they become the focus of the group real quick. People can deal with being uncomfortable only so long until they begin to look for a place where they feel accepted.

The Real Work of the Church

William Raspberry of the *Washington Post* writers group speaking at the annual council of the Episcopal Church in Mississippi issued a challenge for the church to play to its strength. He compared the church to a 7-foot basketball player who prefers to shoot from 15 or 20 feet from the basket or to bring the ball down to his chest which takes away his height advantage.

Speaking about social issues such as feeding the hungry and housing the homeless, he said the church that neglects the spiritual and moral aspects of man is not playing to its strength. In doing so, we are much like the 7-footer who is not playing to his strengths—a big man playing small, as coaches say. This writer from an obviously secular newspaper states:

> Doesn't the neglect of the spiritual at least help explain the persistence not just of homelessness but also teen pregnancy, substance abuse, school failure and the whole range of problems that we tend to see as stemming primarily from bad economics or racism? Shouldn't organized religion take the lead in doing what the rest of us fear to try? (Raspberry, A6).

In the same article, Raspberry quotes Robert L. Woodson, Sr., head of the national center for Neighborhood Enterprise:

> We have been looking for cures in all the wrong places. We don't have a crisis in recreation, or social services, or consumer capacity. Certainly our children need these things, and need jobs too. But these things have no redemptive quality, and what our young people need above all is to be redeemed (A6).

There is a difference between the real work of the church and doing church work. While doing church work, it is easy to get caught in "oiling the church machinery" and forget the real work of the church.

Church work involves its programs, organizations, corporate plans,
etc. The work of the church involves what the members of the
church are doing between Sundays—business, industry, the profes-
sions, education, labor, agriculture, sales, consulting, etc.
(Halverson, June 22, 1994, 1).

Making the shift from dysfunctional to functional requires a no-
compromise position toward the cross of Jesus Christ. Whatever
method is used to reach an addictive society, the foundation must
be the words of the Apostle Paul, "I am not ashamed of the gospel"
(Romans 1:6). People in this society have turned inward for answers
to life's problems to find only emptiness. Jesus Christ is the only
foundation which provides an environment for healing and growth.
"For no one can lay any foundation other than the one already laid,
which is Jesus Christ" (1 Corinthians 3:11).

E-mail, on-line, the worldwide web, virtual reality, the information highway, and "alternative-you-name-it" are common terms as
we move into the third millennium. Cyberspace cannot take the
place of building one another relationships and character. Over 20
years ago, I heard Billy Graham make a statement at First Baptist
Church in Jackson, Mississippi, I will never forget. Speaking to an
audience of pastors and other church leaders, he said on a scale of
1 to 10, you may have the charisma of a 10, the communication
skills of a 9, the biblical knowledge of a 9, and the intelligence of a
10. However, if your character is a 3, your ministry will always grav-
itate to the level of your character.

More advanced technology will never take the place of building
a relationship with Jesus Christ and others. On this foundation we
build character. Peter says, "As you come to him, the living Stone—
rejected by men but chosen by God and precious to him—you also,
like living stones, are being built into a spiritual house to be a holy
priesthood, offering spiritual sacrifices acceptable to God through
Jesus Christ" (1 Peter 2:4-5).

11

$\mathcal{A}$ Biblical Church Model

The Apostle Paul describes the church of the Thessalonians as "a model to all the believers in Macedonia and Achaia" (1Thessalonians 1:7). If Paul chooses to call this church a model, then perhaps we should look closely at what they were doing and his instructions on how we can improve our pattern of ministry.

Paul's first visit to this city was on his second missionary journey (Acts 17:1). In his day, the population of the city was about 200,000. Thessalonica was an important seaport city which made it a strategic trading center. It was on the Egnatian Way which was an important trade and military route between Rome and Asia Minor. This busy and prosperous city was accessible both by land and sea.

The majority of the city's population was Greek although there was a large and influential Jewish presence. When Paul and Silas came to Thessalonica, "As his custom was, Paul went into the synagogue, and on three Sabbath days he reasoned with them from the Scriptures, explaining and proving that the Christ had to suffer and rise from the dead" (Acts 17:2-3). Some of the Jews followed

Christ as did a large number of Greeks. Being jealous, the Jews started a riot and looked for Paul and Silas but could not find them.

Choosing to avoid more trouble, Paul and his companions left Thessalonica. Concerning the chronology of Paul's later contacts with the church, Jensen says:

> (1) Twice Paul was hindered from returning to Thessalonica soon after his first visit (1 Thessalonians 2:17-18), (2) he sent Timothy to minister in his place (1 Thessalonians 3:1-2), (3) he wrote the two epistles, (4) the apostle made at least two other visits to the area on his third missionary journey (Acts 20:1-4; 2 Corinthians 2:12-13) (350).

Since Paul had to leave Thessalonica quickly, there was no support system for the new converts. It is in this context that he writes to them after learning from Timothy about their wonderful progress and the need for further instructions in practical relationships and doctrine.

Being a model church does not mean they were without problems. This church was full of young converts fresh from paganism but eager to follow Christ even though they had their struggles. This paradigm shift from serving idols to serving God is a model which deserves our attention. The principles are applicable for our present addictive society.

It is not that this shift occurred without problems. Coming out of a paganistic society, their morals were very low. A standard of holiness was new to them. Paul told them, "It is God's will that you should be holy; that you should avoid sexual immorality; that each of you should learn to control his own body in a way that is holy and honorable" (1 Thessalonians 4:3-4). Paul dealt with them concerning idleness. He encouraged them "to mind [their] own business and to work with [their] hands" (1 Thessalonians 4:11). Apparently their idleness was causing some to get unduly involved in the business of others.

Paul addressed their misunderstanding regarding the Second Coming of Christ (1 Thessalonians 4:13-17). The Thessalonians

were concerned about those who had already died and their missing the event of meeting "the Lord in the air." Some apparently had
misinterpreted the teaching of the imminence of the Lord's return
as giving warrant for idleness. They may have reasoned, "If He were
coming so soon, why such carefulness as to physical necessities?
Why not just luxuriate in the white robe of divine righteousness and
wait [as some in modern time have done] on some mountain top
for the trumpet to sound? (4:11-12)" (Boyd, 24). Their restlessness
can be contributed to an unhealthy view concerning the coming of
the Lord.

In addition to these problems, the Thessalonians were having to
face the criticisms against Paul which were probably instigated by
Jewish opposition. In this letter, Paul defended his conduct and
character.

The church of the Thessalonians was not removed from problems, trials, and misunderstandings. However, Paul serves notice
that this was a model community of believers. Let's look at some of
the principles involved with this church.

The Church Is in God

Paul opens his letter with these words: "To the church of the
Thessalonians in God the Father and the Lord Jesus Christ" (1
Thessalonians 1:1). Immediately we see a living relationship with
the Father and the Son. John writes, "And our fellowship is with the
Father and with his Son, Jesus Christ" (1 John 1:3). Jesus says: "If
anyone loves me, he will obey my teaching. My Father will love him,
and we will come to him and make our home with him" (John
14:23).

One of the tools of Satan (as discussed in Chapter 5) is isolation
or hiding. Everyone will have a hiding place. Paul describes the
believer's hiding place in Colossians 3:3: "For you died, and your
life is now hidden with Christ in God." The Church is a community
of believers hidden in God. The life in the Church comes from
God. The Church is not a building; it is believers in a living rela-

tionship with Christ. Unfortunately, some so-called churches are "hidden" in the arts, social movements, politics, and denominations. However, many do not know what it is to be "hidden in God."

Have you ever been tempted just to run away from your responsibilities? In Psalm 11:1, David was being encouraged to "flee like a bird to [his] mountain." We all have a mountain we want to flee to at times. David refused the advice. He said, "In the LORD I take refuge." *In God* we have assurance and protection in changing times to serve as our anchor. "Because God wanted to make the unchanging nature of his purpose very clear to the heirs of what was promised, he confirmed it with an oath. . . . We have this hope as an anchor for the soul, firm and secure" (Hebrews 6:17,19).

The Church Is Known by Faith, Love, and Hope

Paul commends the church. "We continually remember before our God and Father your work produced by faith, your labor prompted by love, and your endurance inspired by hope in our Lord Jesus Christ" (1 Thessalonians 1:3). This triad of faith, love and hope is found in other passages in the New Testament. The often quoted love chapter, 1 Corinthians 13, concludes with "faith, hope and love" (v13).

John Stott says: "Each is outgoing. Faith is directed towards God, love towards others (both within the Christian fellowship and beyond it), and hope towards the future, in particular the glorious coming of our Lord Jesus Christ" (29-30). Being *in God*, the Thes - salonians had faith that was based on Jesus Christ. Their faith was more than an intellectual exercise; it produced action. The action was a labor of love. Faith *in God* helps us to work diligently through love for people who are not lovable or who seem to be undeserving of our love. Growing faith is always an indication of life and a healthy walk with Christ. This faith results in an overflowing of love towards others.

The believers at Thessalonica were able to endure because they had hope. Their hope was in Christ and His return. Although some had a misunderstanding about the second coming of Christ, they were a dynamic church with great expectations. Frank M. Boyd suggests a thematic method concerning hope as presented by Robert Lee of London:

> The Lord's coming an inspiring hope for the young convert (Ch. 1).
> The Lord's coming an encouraging hope for the faithful servant (2 to 3:11).
> The Lord's coming a purifying hope for the believer (3:12 to 4:12).
> The Lord's coming a comforting hope for the bereaved (4:13-18).
> The Lord's coming a rousing hope for the sleepy Christian (Ch. 5) (19).

Love is cradled by faith and hope. Our faith and hope are built around the love of God. "Whoever does not love does not know God, because God is love" (1 John 4:8). This kind of love labors. It goes the second mile. Even our works of faith are based on God's love. Paul says, "At just the right time, when we were still powerless, Christ died for the ungodly. . . . But God demonstrates his own love for us in this: While we were still sinners, Christ died for us" (Romans 5:6, 8). And because of God's love, we have hope that will not disappoint us "because God has poured out his love into our hearts by the Holy Spirit, whom he has given us" (Romans 5:5). As love labors, faith works and hope endures.

The Church Embraces the Gospel

Being chosen and loved by God, the Thessalonians received the "message with joy." The message was the gospel. Paul talks about the importance and definition of the gospel: "For what I received I passed on to you as of first importance: that Christ died for our sins according to the Scriptures, that he was buried, that he was raised on the third day according to the Scriptures" (1 Corinthians 15:3-4).

Speaking to the Thessalonians, Paul said, "Our gospel came to you not simply with words, but also with power, with the Holy Spirit"

(1 Thessalonians 1:5). The Holy Spirit reinforces the Word of God. The important balance of the Word of God and the Spirit of God is emphasized by an old preacher who said, "A church with all emphasis on the Spirit will **blow up**. With only concern for the Word, void of the Spirit, the congregation will **dry up**. With both Spirit and Word of God, the church will **grow up**."

When the Word and the Spirit of God are emphasized, the result will be "deep conviction" (v5). The Word of God penetrates man's heart through the power of the Holy Spirit. "We must never divorce what God has married, namely his Word and his Spirit. The Word of God is the Spirit's sword (Ephesians 6:17). The Spirit without the Word is weaponless; the Word without the Spirit is powerless" (Stott, 34).

Evidence that the church of the Thessalonians embraced the gospel is seen in that they became followers of Paul and Christ. Commending the believers, Paul said, "You became imitators of us and of the Lord" (1 Thessalonians 1:6). They followed Paul and Christ "in spite of severe suffering" (v6). These young believers had courage in the midst of persecution. They had the willingness of mind to act out of conviction rather than emotion.

There is a difference between convictions and preferences. Convictions are those things in which we believe so strongly we would give our life for them. This addictive society is looking for the community of believers to stand up for strong convictions. This is especially true since this society advocates *tolerance* toward ungodly behavior. William Penn said: "Right is right, even if everyone is against it, and wrong is wrong, even if everyone is for it" (Tan, 283).

The Church Is a Model to All

An important part of this paradigm is the church at Thessalonica's comprehensive evangelism focus. Notice how the gospel progressed with them. First, the gospel came to them. Next, they "welcomed the message with joy." Then the "message rang out [from them] not only in Macedonia and Achaia—[their] faith in God has become known everywhere" (v8).

Their message concerning Christ rang loudly and clearly and continued to ring. Their faith in God became "known everywhere" (v8), not only in Macedonia and Achaia. Much can be said about media evangelism; however, the Thessalonians did not have television, radio, tapes, or cyberspace. They used the most effective evangelism—one-on-one. They used the strategic location of Thessalonica to their advantage. Being on the Egnatian Way which was a major route between Rome and Asia minor provided them with access to travelers all over the Roman Empire. So effective were the Thessalonians' evangelism efforts that travelers throughout the Roman Empire reported to Paul the message of the Thessalonians.

The Church Turns to God from Idols

There was testimony of true repentance among this model community of believers. "They tell how you turned to God from idols to serve the living and true God, and to wait for his Son from heaven, whom he raised from the dead—Jesus" (vv9-10). The turn was not just switching religious affiliations, switching denominational affiliations, or the changing of opinion by pagans, this turn was evidenced by changed lives. They had turned to God from idols.

Why was this change so radical yet wise? John Stott says, "Idols are dead; God is living. Idols are false; God is true. Idols are many; God is one. Idols are visible and tangible; God is invisible and intangible, beyond the reach of sight and touch. Idols are creatures, the work of human hands; God is the Creator of the universe and of all humankind" (39). This evangelism focus did more than report numbers. Instead, they reported changed lives—"They tell how you turned to God from idols" (v9).

The Thessalonians not only turned from, but they also turned to. God always replaces the idols which are God-substitutes with the real thing. A person without a relationship with Jesus Christ is always searching to fill the void with a God-substitute. Merril C. Tenney says, "Paganism is the human attempt to satisfy an inner longing for God by the worship of a deity which will not obstruct one's desire for self-satisfaction" (107-108). The book of Ecclesiastes describes man without a proper relationship with God: " 'Meaningless! Mean-

ingless!' " says the Teacher. 'Utterly meaningless! Everything is
meaningless' " (Ecclesiastes 1:2). Without God, life is hollow, empty,
and without purpose.

It is common for people who have been in the grips of life-controlling substances, behaviors, or relationships to feel a void in their
life when they start the road to freedom. Dr. Abraham Twerski says,
"Although almost every human disease can be found among animals, there is no evidence that animals in their normal habitat
develop addictive diseases. . . . In contrast to animals, which have
only physical urges and desires, human beings crave spiritual fulfillment as well" (91). What is the difference between humans and
animals? Humans have a spirit. Animals do not. Therefore, the vacuum is a spiritual void.

The church at Thessalonica turned to the only source that could
fill the void left by their heathenism. They "turned to God . . . to
serve the living and true God" (1 Thessalonians 1:9). Just turning
from mastering idols is essential but not enough. When the God-
void is not filled, many people in recovery will go to another addiction to fill the void of the one they were battling. Speaking to the
Ephesian elders, Paul shows that confession and repentance are
essential. However, he said, "both Jews and Greeks . . . must turn to
God in repentance and *have faith in our Lord Jesus*" (Acts 20:21)
(emphasis added).

Not only were the Thessalonians turning to the true God, but
they were also serving the living God. Idols produce no life. They
always move a person into a downward spiral. John writes, "He who
has the Son has life; he who does not have the Son of God does not
have life" (1 John 5:12).

This church was an active, dynamic, and expectant group of
believers. They were waiting for God's "Son from heaven, whom he
raised from the dead" (1 Thessalonians 1:10). The resurrection of
Christ was the center of their commitment to the gospel. Christ's
resurrection provided the hope they needed as they waited as well
as the assurance that believers would be resurrected (1 Corinthians
15:20).

The Thessalonians were known for their faith, love, and hope. Characteristics of this triad are: "work produced by faith"—"turned to God from idols"; "labor prompted by love"—"to serve the living and true God; "endurance inspired by hope"—"to wait for his Son from heaven" (1:3, 9-10).

In Chapter 5, we discussed the three primary resources of God and how they combat the three common tools used by Satan in this addictive society: delusion, isolation, and hiding. The church at Thessalonica used God's resources. The church of the Thessalonians is an example of the Word of God, the Spirit of God, and the people of God working together. Although far from being a perfect church, it is described as "a model to all the believers in Macedonia and Achaia" (1:7). They "welcomed the message" [the word of God] (1:6). The word came "with power, with the Holy Spirit" [the Spirit of God] (1:5). The Thessalonians recognized that Paul and Silas lived the life because they "lived among" them for their sake [the people of God] (1:5).

Building a relationship with Christ and with one another is the way to live in the pressures of a paganistic society. Let us stand on the promises of the Word, be guided by the Holy Spirit, and care for one another in the family of God. Speaking to this family of God, Paul says, "We were gentle among you, like a mother caring for her little children. We loved you so much that we were delighted to share with you not only the gospel of God but our lives as well" (1 Thessalonians 2:7-8). He describes the father relationship as one of "encouraging, comforting and urging" (1 Thessalonians 2:12). As the people of God we can encourage one another—offering gentleness always and firmness when needed.

12

Small Groups: A Paradigm for Christian Community

Over the last several years, the Church and society have seen a distinct increase in the small group movement. Many agree the reason for this has been the societal changes of the past few decades. Our society has become an addicted society—addicted to substances, behaviors, and relationships. People in today's society struggle to cope with drug abuse, sexual abuse, family fragmentation, loneliness, lack of community closeness, high crime, and numerous other difficult problems. A longing for meaningful relationships is prevalent. The Church can be the agent through which this longing can be filled. Small groups can provide a nonthreatening environment where people can build trust in each other and help each other deal with his/her own struggles.

In the Church, small groups can be far more effective than in a secular setting. In Christ-centered small groups which have a specific curriculum and focus, an atmosphere for spiritual healing and growth is prevalent because the gospel of Jesus Christ, the power of the Holy Spirit, and insight from Scripture can be presented. Small groups can also be a tremendous evangelism tool as the Church presents the Gospel to those who are seeking help.

150

A group can have a significant influence, positive or negative, on its individual members. Social psychologists define a group as a collection of people who interact regularly in fairly structured and predictable ways, who are oriented toward one or more specific goals which are aimed at satisfying certain shared needs, and who have a feeling of group identity and solidarity. They feel themselves a part of the whole, sharing a common fate.

Small groups have a strong element of peer pressure because of regular interaction and orientation toward specific goals. However, when Christ is not the center, the peer power of the group can be negative. People can be led to look to something, someone, or their own selves as their higher power. One story that illustrates the negative power is about a young college student who was a political activist on her college campus. Being politically radical, she was even into trying to overthrow the system of government at the school. However, during this time, she joined a religious cult group on campus and shortly thereafter, to the surprise of her family, underwent a drastic personality change. The girl who had been so strong-willed and independent became meek and obedient. Within three months, she was obeying everyone to the extreme, even to the point of giving herself to any guy who demanded she do so. For four years she lived under the influence of this group.

Although small group influence without proper direction can be abusive, there is a positive influence when Christ is the focus that can bring people to wholeness. I have heard many testimonies from people who have received Christ as Savior, had their marriages miraculously put back together, had suicides prevented, addictions broken, etc., as a result of the positive influence the Christ-centered small group had on their lives.

John Wesley (1703-1791) had a fervent ministry of evangelism which addressed social concerns through small groups. Wesley had a highly organized system of group life including these groups: society, class meeting, band, select society and pertinent band. These groups provided group experience at various levels. Although Wesley received much criticism about his emphasis on confession, "Confess your sins to each other" (James 5:16) continued to be one of his most quoted scripture verses. These were meetings of small groups of people for the purpose of prayer, reading, and sharing.

Frank Buchman (1878-1961), a Lutheran minister, was the founder of the Oxford Group movement (later known as Moral Rearmament) which spread rapidly. Although he was very controversial, his impact on Christianity in the twentieth century cannot be denied. Buchman believed the greatest hindrance in a person's knowing God was the appetites of the flesh. His concept was that everyone was in need of change and people should meet together for confessions and prayer. His principles of change were instrumental in the starting of the Alcoholics Anonymous movement.

Garth Lean in his book, *On the Tail of a Comet,* writes extensively about the life of Frank Buchman. "The early AA got its ideas of self-examination, acknowledgment of character defects, restitution for harm done, and working with others, straight from the Oxford Groups and directly from Sam Shoemaker . . . and from nowhere else" (152). Shoemaker experienced a change of life through Buchman's ministry which started a 20-year association. Shoemaker later had an effective ministry to alcoholics at Calvary Church in New York City.

Lean further quotes Paul Tournier, the Swiss psychiatrist, regarding Buchman's effect on the church. "Before Buchman the church felt its job was to teach and preach, but not to find out what was happening in people's souls. The clergy never listened in church, they always talked" (153). Many spin-off movements dealing with social ills have found their roots in the AA movement where Buchman's ideas were so influential.

Sunday school became the dominant small group movement in the late 1800s. Because it was not limited to a single denomination, it had a broader effect than did the Wesley group meetings. Lyman Coleman says, "By 1950, 75 percent of church members were involved in Sunday school . . . by 1970 Sunday school with its emphasis on age category, on-site location and Sunday-only meetings was clearly in decline" (Bird, 27). However, the small group idea was moving to the forefront as a result of the emphasis on life issues, flexibility of meeting sites, and days.

The small group has been through some dramatic changes over the past two decades and is hard to define; nonetheless, it is meeting a core need in today's society. Small groups are popular in many different denominations, areas, and classes of people; therefore, churches can be flexible in responding to the various needs of its community. In recent years we have seen Sunday schools become more small-group oriented and addressing felt needs. John Vaughan, professor of church growth at Southwest Baptist Seminary, Bolivar, Missouri, asserts that even though small groups play a strategic role in the assimilation and equipping ministry and that most large churches survive through instituting small groups effectively, Sunday school should still be emphasized. "He notes that some churches emphasize home groups, some Sunday school, but only a few do both well" (Bird, 28-29).

> Overall, the small-group movement cannot be understood except in relation to the deep yearning for the sacred that characterized much of the American public. Indeed, a great deal of the momentum for the movement as a whole comes from the fact that people are interested in spirituality, on the one hand, and from the availability of vast resources from religious organizations, on the other. As a result, small groups are dramatically redefining how Americans think about God" (Wuthnow, 23-24).

There is a spiritual vacuum and hunger for meaningful relationships in this addictive society. A church that is prepared for the future must have a healthy combination of corporate worship of God and small groups which focus on relationships and felt needs.

Long before small groups were a popular trend, the Apostle Paul wrote about the church filling the role as a caring community (Ephesians 4).

> The church is an evangelizing, preaching, teaching, discipling, sending community. It also must be a therapeutic community where

people find love, acceptance, forgiveness, support, hope, encouragement, burden-bearing, caring, meaning, opportunities for service, challenge, and help in times of need. Within the church community, people can find others who share "like precious faith" and
who value the spiritual issues that secular therapists so often overlook (Collins, 1986, 30).

With the breakdown of the family, many people are without
mothers, fathers, brothers, and sisters. Small groups provide family
ties and assistance in developing one another relationships.
Breaking through the isolation and pain, "God sets the lonely in
families" (Psalm 68:6).

The Christ-Centered Small Group

The wheel on page 156 represents a Christ-centered small group.
The spokes are the group members, and Christ is the hub. As the
group members come near Christ, the hub, they also develop a
closeness with one another.

Lack of personal growth is often seen in small groups when a
group member's problem, the group leader, or a philosophy
becomes the center. Although sharing of struggles is good, if given
center stage in the small group, it may cause group members to
become manipulative, selfish, and/or irresponsible which will cause
confusion. They may learn to cope but will rarely come to a point of
healing.

When the group leader becomes the center of the small group—
the spiritual or psychological guru—group members may form a
dependent relationship with him/her. Group leaders should stand
with (or hand in hand with) group members but not as lord. Paul
writes, "Not that we lord it over your faith, but we work with you for
your joy, because it is by faith you stand firm" (2 Corinthians 1:24-
2:1).

If a philosophy becomes the center of the small group, an emptiness or even deception among group members is the likely result.
Philosophies that mislead groups include intellectualism, specula-

tions, or good-sounding arguments that neglect Christ as being pre-eminent. "See to it that no one takes you captive through hollow and deceptive philosophy, which depends on human tradition and the basic principles of this world rather than on Christ" (Colossians 2:8).

> The sounds which come from an empty head will reveal its hollow-ness. After delivering a sermon, grandpa was approached by an "educated" visitor who wanted to correct his language. He began: "You used the phrase aching void. I wish you would tell me how a void can ache."

> "Well, not to speak of a hollow tooth, don't you sometimes have the headache?" was grandpa's silencer (Brownlow, 28).

So then, what is a Christ-centered small group? Through all dis-cussions (pain, victories, misunderstandings, anger, opinions, frus-trations, etc.), it is the responsibility of the leader to bring the dis-cussion back to a personal level that focuses on Jesus Christ. "Let us fix our eyes on Jesus, the author and perfecter of our faith, who for the joy set before him endured the cross, scorning its shame, and sat down at the right hand of the throne of God" (Hebrews 12:2).

Construct a poster board using the Christ-centered wheel. Place a group member's name on each spoke with Christ as the hub. The leader and co-leader will be identified as spokes also. Place the wheel on the wall where it can be referred to regularly.

To help the group stay focused, it is important to follow a bibli-cally based curriculum. God's "word is a lamp to my feet and a light for my path" (Psalm 119:105). The Word as a lamp shows specific steps for our feet. The Word as light provides general direction for the path. As in an automobile, we may not be able to see beyond our headlights, but we still get to our destination.

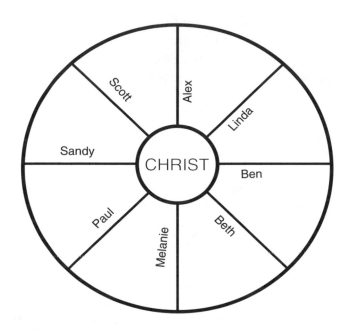

Figure 12-1

A Biblical Perspective for Small Groups

In the book of Galatians the Apostle Paul gives considerable time to refuting the teaching of the Judaizers. They were trying to convince the new converts that faith in Christ alone was not enough. They urged the new Christians to keep the Mosiac law by being circumcised (Galatians 5:2-6). Paul maintains that mixing the law with faith is not the means of salvation.

Paul emphasizes freedom in Christ: "You, my brothers, were called to be free. But do not use your freedom to indulge the sinful nature; rather, serve one another in love" (Galatians 5:13). Although this book was written to the churches in Galatia, Paul often talks in terms such as brethren and one another. "Since we live by the Spirit, let us keep in step with the Spirit. Let us not be conceited, provoking and envying each other" (Galatians 5:25-26).

The goal of small groups is to help each other "keep in step with the Spirit." Instead of becoming conceited, provocative, and envious, helpers are encouraged to treat their brothers and sisters with love and concern. In Galatians 6:1-5, Paul presents principles that will help any small group leader as he or she helps others overcome obstacles that may hinder a person's freedom in Christ.

Help for the Trapped

"Brothers, if someone is caught in a sin . . . " (Galatians 6:1). Note that Paul looks to the brothers for help. This could also refer to brothers and sisters in Christ. Someone has taken a "false step." The person has been trapped, overtaken by a sin. Perhaps they need the help to which Hebrews 12:1 refers: "Let us throw off everything that hinders and the sin that so easily entangles."

Kennon L. Callahan says that "most new members join a church longing for and looking for help, hope, and home" (213). People who have been overtaken by a sin are sitting in churches but are afraid to come forward. This verse places on the believer the responsibility of helping his fellow believer. Creating an atmosphere of understanding for the entire church (the 20-60-20 referred to in Chapter 10) will free people to help others become free.

Helped Helpers. "You who are spiritual should restore him gently" (Galatians 6:1). Those who are noncarnal are the spiritual helpers. Paul says in 1 Corinthians 3:1, "Brothers, I could not address you as spiritual but as worldly—mere infants in Christ." Unhelped helpers often transfer their baggage to other people. Some small groups led by unhelped helpers often go in circles without purpose. One such group was a codependent group of ladies that has met for six years. The same ladies rehashed the same problems each week. Such groups can cause harm to its members because they learn unhelped behaviors from unhelped helpers.

Being a helped helper does not mean a perfect helper or a helper without problems. The helped helper is aware of his baggage and is working on it. The helper is helping his fellow believers focus on Christ instead of the baggage. David had his struggles—family problems, adultery, and murder. David said, "My sin is always before me" (Psalm 51:3). Far from being perfect or without problems, David had a heart for God (Acts 13:22). Without question, David was a helped helper.

The method of help is gentle restoration. Paul's instruction is to "restore him gently." To restore means to set the bones or mend the nets. Another way to look at restoration is to help a person put the parts back together in his or her life. A gentle touch is needed much like a nurse's providing physical therapy to a person recovering from a broken limb.

Humble Helpers. "But watch yourself, or you may also be tempted" (Galatians 6:1). This verse warns against the conceit that is mentioned in Galatians 5:26. An arrogant, overconfident, or self-proclaimed spiritual giant goes against the atmosphere of surrender so badly needed in a small group. "Do not think of yourself more highly than you ought, but rather think of yourself with sober judgment, in accordance with the measure of faith God has given you" (Romans 12:3).

Humble helpers will not scold the weak or work to develop the group around themselves. These helpers do not point their finger or glory in the failings of others. They understand it is only by the grace of God that it is not they. God gives grace and exalts the humble helper. Being a humble helper is not to be confused with being a weak person. Paul writes, "For when I am weak, then I am strong" (2 Corinthians 12:10).

Hand-in-hand helpers. "Carry each other's burdens, and in this way you will fulfill the law of Christ" (Galatians 6:2). Paul emphasizes the responsibility of the believer to the fellow believer who has taken a "false step." The goal is to help the fallen person place their dependence upon the Spirit of God. We are to "accept him whose faith is weak, without passing judgment on disputable matters" (Romans 14:1).

Paul is concerned for the Galatians because they were placing themselves back under legalism. He said to them, "After beginning with the Spirit, are you now trying to attain your goal by human effort" (Galatians 3:3)? Now he is calling for the brothers and sisters to be hand-in-hand helpers by assisting with the burdens of fellow believers. We are to "rejoice with those who rejoice; mourn with those who mourn. Live in harmony with one another" (Romans 12:15-16).

A hand-in-hand helper does not take personal responsibility from others. The helper should avoid dominating other people. Caution must be taken because some people who are dependent on any type of authority figure will cling to the helper. Paul states, "Not that we lord it over your faith, but we work with you for your joy, because it is by faith you stand firm" (2 Corinthians 1:24-2:1). We should not force-feed people with instructions, Scripture, or even Jesus Christ. Our work is to stand with them—not independent of one another (independence) or leaning on one another to the point that when one falls, the other does also (codependency) but standing together as hand-in-hand helpers and in so doing "fulfill the law of Christ" (Galatians 6:2). Jesus said, "A new command I give you: Love one another. As I have loved you, so you must love one another" (John 13:34).

Helper Traps

Sometimes helpers are less effective because of their own dys-functional background, distorted views of God, and personal mis-beliefs. With this in mind, it is easy for layworkers, pastors, coun-selors, and group leaders to fall unknowingly into helper traps. Galatians 6:3-5 provides awareness for common traps faced by most helpers.

Delusion. "If anyone thinks he is something when he is nothing, he deceives himself" (Galatians 6:3). Feeling spiritually or morally superior to those receiving help is a sure way to deceive one's self. Sober thinking reminds us to watch ourselves closely, or we "may be tempted." Concerning conceit, David writes: "For in his own eyes he flatters himself too much to detect or hate his sin" (Psalm 36:2). The Pharisees were known for their self-righteousness. "The Pharisee stood up and prayed about himself: 'God, I thank you that

I am not like all other men—robbers, evildoers, adulterers—or even like this tax collector' " (Luke 18:11). Such conceit eliminates a person as a helper. Pride results in delusion. Jeremiah writes, "The pride of your heart [has] deceived you" (49:16).

Lack of self-examination. "Each one should test his own actions" (Galatians 6:4). A helper must always examine himself first. Are you in a right relationship with God? What about your attitude, your motives? An examination of yourself can help prevent conceit and pride which leads to deluded thinking. True examination helps a person recognize that he or she is nothing without God. "Let him who boasts boast in the Lord" (1 Corinthians 1:31).

An effective small group leader will join other group members in self-examination. True examination will show that we all have weaknesses—laypeople, pastors, counselors, and denominational leaders. "So, if you think you are standing firm, be careful that you don't fall" (1 Corinthians 10:12)!

Lack of self-esteem. "Then he can take pride in himself" (Galatians 6:4). The correct kind of pride is not an excessive or unjustified evaluation of one's self; instead, the grounds for our boasting are through the Holy Spirit. Our true identity is in Jesus Christ. Many have an identity problem because their identity is in their church affiliation, ethnic pride, code of morals, or social status. C. S. Lewis says:

> It is no good trying to "be myself" without Him. The more I resist Him and try to live on my own, the more I become dominated by my own heredity and upbringing and surroundings and natural desires. In fact what I so proudly call "Myself" becomes merely the meeting place for trains of events which I never started and which I cannot stop (189).

Don Matzat, author of the popular book, *Christ Esteem,* describes our need as Christ esteem, not self-esteem. It is amazing what will happen when we quit focusing on our self and esteem Christ. Paul writes, "And he died for all, that those who live should no longer live for themselves, but for him who died for them and was raised again" (2 Corinthians 5:15).

A friend once told me about his difficulty in receiving compliments. When he received a compliment in his early walk with Christ, he would say with a pious ring, "It's not me, it's Jesus." He then graduated simply to pointing with his finger in the air, "one way." He finally realized he only needed to say thank you to the one giving the compliment. Then at night before he went to bed, he would thank God for using him.

Approval trap. "Without comparing himself to someone else" (Galatians 6:4). Our character, commitment, and effectiveness in the Lord is to be tested in the light of God's approval. It is easy to get caught in the approval trap by comparing ourselves to others. Being approved by God is based on a solid foundation; whereas, the approval of others is relative because it is based on imperfect people.

I have seen well-meaning believers try to sing like certain Christian artists, preach with the same mannerisms as a TV preacher, or copy the latest Christian fad in order to meet the approval of others. Being "in Christ" makes each believer unique in Christ.

> Sameness is to be found most among the most 'natural' men, not among those who surrender to Christ. . . . Look for yourself, and you will find in the long run only hatred, loneliness, despair, rage, ruin, and decay. But look for Christ and you will find him, and with Him everything else thrown in (Lewis, 190).

Lack of Personal Responsibility. "For each one should carry his own load" (Galatians 6:5). People often claim contradiction between this verse and "carry each other's burdens" in verse 2. Instead, these two verses provide a balance in being a people helper. Yes, we are to "carry each other's burdens," but there are some loads that only God and you can carry. This verse emphasizes personal responsibility. Everyone is responsible to God for who he or she is and for their own actions. As helpers, we are to offer a helping hand but not take away one's own personal responsibility to carry his or her own load. Our own load is those private, personal burdens that only we and God can carry. "Continue to work out your salvation with fear and trembling, for it is God who works in you to will and to act according to his good purpose" (Philippians 2:12-13).

The Value of Small Groups

Small groups are an effective tool that should be used in a local church model for the hurting. Over the past several years, I have observed the value of people meeting together to deal with their struggles. J. Keith Miller states:

> The question immediately came up in my mind (and often comes up when people are considering joining such a group): Can people with no theological or psychological training really help each other overcome serious character defects? For years I would have said no. But as I have participated in and watched groups operate over the years I have come to realize that a group of ordinary people trying to surrender their lives to God and discover that their own denial and delusion with rigorous honesty can often give amazingly effective help with real-life difficulties (207).

Small groups are a way to offer Christian love and support. People are in search of *meaningful relationships*. With Christ as the center of small groups, a therapy can be provided that is not otherwise available. The ultimate therapist is the Holy Spirit.

Loneliness is one of the major problems of our society. Many people are no more than numbers on their jobs. Since a large number of people move from their homes yearly, friendships among neighbors are not likely to be established. With less emphasis on community schools and get-togethers, people feel more isolated. A person may go to church every Sunday without really knowing the others who sit in the same pew. That person may be carrying hurts no one knows about or much less understands.

Small group ministry can address the problem of loneliness which is even more prevalent among those struggling with life-controlling problems. God deals with man's need for relationships very early in the Bible: "It is not good for the man to be alone" (Genesis 2:18). The Book of Hebrews, which is addressed primarily to Jewish Christians who were tempted to return to Judaism or mix Judaism with the gospel, deals with two important relationships in Chapter 10:19-25. In verses 19-23, the author shows the important need for a relationship with God which is provided by the blood of Jesus. In verses 24-25, the author discusses the need for a relationship with each other:

> And let us consider how we may spur [incite, provoke] one another on toward love and good deeds. Let us not give up meeting together, as some are in the habit of doing, but let us encourage one another.

Small group ministry is not a new concept. Jesus and his twelve disciples are a paradigm for Christian community. Jesus' regular meetings with his twelve disciples are a clear example of a small group at work. Not only did the disciples benefit from this experience, but Jesus also received close fellowship with this group. "He appointed twelve—designating them apostles—that they might be with him and he might send them out to preach" (Mark 3:14). It is no accident that twelve people or less is suggested for small group participation.

Christians have met together for almost two thousand years with Christ as the focus and the Bible as the road map. These fellowships have included bible studies and prayer. Christians have met in homes, churches, and catacombs. Small groups were active in the New Testament Church (*see* Acts 2:41-47). Small groups are not to take the place of corporate worship; their function is to complement the assembly worship. Corporate worship and small groups can provide an environment for spiritual healing and growth. Small groups where Christ is the focus are Christian community. When the church is the spiritual hospital, small groups can be the support unit of the church. Small groups worked together with corporate worship in the New Testament for healthy growth. Luke writes in

Acts 2:47 they were "praising God and enjoying the favor of all the people. And the Lord added to their number daily those who were being saved." Church history records that many of our modern-day denominations originated from small-group ministries.

Small groups can provide a nonthreatening environment for people to receive help in dealing with their life-controlling problems, a place for them to take a look at themselves and focus on practical steps to grow in Christ. Small groups allow a person to be himself or herself, to take off masks, to receive encouragement, to develop accountability to Christ and to one another. According to *Newsweek* (February 5, 1990):

> A 10-year study by researchers at Stanford University showed that terminally ill cancer patients who participated in weekly support-group meetings in addition to receiving treatment lived nearly twice as long as those receiving only medical care (Leerhsen and Namuth, 52).

In small groups, individual prayer and affirmation personalizes ministry. "Therefore confess your sins to each other and pray for each other so that you may be healed. The prayer of a righteous man is powerful and effective" (James 5:16). "We need small groups because they help us to become what we are meant to be—those set free by the love of Christ, who seek to share his love with others" (Hestenes, 10).

Small groups are one of the most effective ways to deal with delusion. In an atmosphere of surrender to the Lord, the Holy Spirit and Word of God help people see themselves more clearly (*see* Psalm 139:23-24; Hebrews 4:12-13). God also uses believers to help each other expose delusion through encouragement. "But encourage one another daily, as long as it is called Today, so that none of you may be hardened by sin's deceitfulness" (Hebrews 3:13).

Characteristics of Effective Small Groups

Effective small groups are characterized by Christ's being the *center* of the group. Having a bonding of ideas is good; however, unless

Christ is the center, lives will not be transformed. An effective group will be committed to each member and have respect for the claims of Christ.

Commitment to each other means faithfulness in meeting attendance, participation by members, and adherence to confidentiality. In an effective group, each group member will be committed to pray for other group members. Group members take ownership of their feelings without putting others down; they learn to take a look at their own defenses that may be protecting them from the truth.

Effective small groups depend heavily on the group facilitators (leaders). It is suggested that each group have two facilitators. One should take the lead in the meeting and the other should assist in offering input into the group process. The facilitators should work to create an atmosphere for openness and acceptance. Healthy groups develop deep, caring relationships. "One of the basic working assumptions of all group therapies is that human relationships are not only important but also essential for healthy functioning" (Benner, 319). An effective group experiences learning and growth because Christ, not the group leader or any group member, is the center.

There was a time when aggressive confrontation techniques were used in an attempt to break through a person's delusion. Small groups do not need *four-letter words, shouting,* or a *tear 'em down* philosophy to be effective. Groups that are effective recognize the value of a Christ-centered environment where there are no putdowns; instead, there are respect, nurturing, and careful confrontation.

The Role of Group Facilitators

The role of group facilitators is crucial to the success of groups aimed at helping people in this dysfunctional society. The group facilitator and co-facilitator lead the group members, using the appropriate curriculum, through various group dynamics that will change their view of themselves and their world.

There are two things a small group leader should remember. First, God does not expect the leader to have all the answers or work miracles in the lives of group members. That is God's work. Instead, the leader should simply guide the group toward the healing and solutions which the Holy Spirit provides—God will do the rest. Second, leaders should remember that Christian small groups are quite different from secular ones. Secular groups attempt to bring about behavior modification through peer pressure and group dynamics. Although there is a place for positive peer pressure and group dynamics in the Christian small group, there must be a change in the heart. "Godly sorrow brings repentance that leads to salvation and leaves no regret, but worldly sorrow brings death" (2 Corinthians 7:10). *Behavior modification* is only a temporary, superficial solution. God offers deeper, long-lasting change through His body—in this case, the small group. To bring that about, the leader must discern the heart of a person's problem and point the sufferer to Christ. In a sense the group leader needs only to *get the ball rolling.*

Healing through the group process will take place naturally. "For where two or three come together in my name, there am I with them" (Matthew 18:20). Group leaders should be aware of some *dos* and *don'ts* that are important for creating an environment of healing and growth.

Dos. Open each group session with prayer remembering to keep Christ as the center throughout the meeting. The main role of the group leader and co-leader is to keep the process going. Although active listening is important, the group leaders should be willing to share their own feelings. This creates warmth and trust which helps group members to feel safe in sharing their feelings.

Care-fronting should always be done with respect and sensitivity. Arrange the chairs so members can easily see each other. Having eye contact will help the interaction. Discussion can be enhanced by open-ended questions. Some examples would be: "Could it be that . . . " "It sounds like . . . " "I hear you saying . . . "

The group leaders should have a sense of humor. It is easy to get caught up in the seriousness of one another's needs and forget the value of laughter. "A cheerful heart is good medicine, but a crushed spirit dries up the bones" (Proverbs 17:22). Humor can enhance the group experience by breaking tension and building trust. Having sensitivity to the timing of humor is important.

Group leaders should have respect for time limitations. The announced time period should be followed. Group members should be respected by the leader's starting and concluding the group session on time. Adherence to the agreed time will build respect for the facilitators. It also helps group members to practice discipline as they commit to the time frame of the group.

Group facilitators should always work within their limitations. When the facilitators see an apparent need for professional counseling for a group member, this does not mean that the group leaders have failed nor does it imply that God's power is insufficient. Instead it should be seen as positive because the individual's need has surfaced. In this case the group leaders should ask for pastoral help in determining the most appropriate Christian service available. Each group member's comfort level should always be respected.

Don'ts. Although therapy occurs in Christian small groups led by non-credentialed group facilitators, group therapy, in the professional sense, should not be attempted. Serving as channels of Christ's love to those who are hurting and desire wholeness in Christ is the purpose. Facilitators should not feel it necessary to solve people's problems; instead, they should create an environment in which the Holy Spirit can do His work.

Avoid probing. Probing may open deep emotional wounds with which the facilitators are not prepared to deal. Group members should be encouraged to share their feelings with the understanding that they should not go beyond their comfort level. "Cast all your anxiety on him because he cares for you" (1 Peter 5:7). Group facilitators should not interpret group members; instead, they should reflect what they say. Counselors who practice group therapy often interpret group members; however, group dynamics is supportive interaction between group members.

Facilitators should not give advice. If the advice given by the helper does not work, the group member may hold the person responsible. Advice may hinder the growth process since the group members may become dependent on the group leaders for insight; whereas, active listening assists the individual with a better understanding of self. If a group member seeks advice from a facilitator, the answer should be general and not violate biblical principles. Becoming a caretaker or accumulating and owning other people's problems is not healthy for the leader or group member. If a group member discloses information that causes the group leader or members to feel uncomfortable, it may be appropriate for the facilitator to request a private meeting at a later time. Facilitators should not feel they must have all the answers or dominate the group discussion.

Discourage gossip. Since it is a sin, gossip should not be a part of any group activity. In the early church, gossip was condemned and associated with other sins (Romans 1:29, 2 Corinthians 12:20). Gossip will destroy a small group.

Qualities of Effective Group Facilitators

Having the spirit of a servant is essential for group leaders. Small groups should not be used as a platform for building the leader's ego. Leaders must guard against possessiveness toward group members or manipulation of those who may be spiritually weak. Christ, not the group leaders, should remain the focus. A servant's heart can be exhibited by encouraging group members to become all God intended them to be.

Having a good attitude is essential to being an effective group leader. A bad attitude will spread among group members and destroy the purpose of the group. The leader's life should exhibit gentleness, purity, and a loving spirit. Positive attitudes can be as contagious as negative attitudes. Submissiveness to the local church is a quality that is needed for all group leaders. Without submissiveness to each other and Christ, groups will do more harm than good. "Submit to one another out of reverence for Christ" (Ephesians 5:21).

Spiritual maturity. Group leaders should have a Bible-based foundation. "All Scripture is God-breathed and is useful for teaching, rebuking, correcting and training in righteousness" (2 Timothy 3:16). Having a good knowledge of the Scripture (*see* 2 Timothy 2:15) along with Bible-based common sense is extremely important. The groups should be led by individuals who are not recent converts (*see* 1 Timothy 3:6). To avoid possible pitfalls, group leaders should be people of proven character. "He must also have a good reputation with outsiders, so that he will not fall into disgrace and into the devil's trap" (1 Timothy 3:7). They should have strong commitment which displays reliability, faithfulness, and follow-through. Spiritual maturity, gentleness, and humility are a special combination for group leaders.

Emotional stability. Group leaders should exhibit a balanced lifestyle with confidence, however, not arrogance or overconfidence. "For God did not give us the spirit of timidity, but a spirit of power, of love and of self-discipline" (2 Timothy 1:7). Those who cannot discipline their own lives will not be effective in leading others to wholeness in Christ. Leaders should be team players, flexible, and adaptable.

Being responsible people, they should speak and work in reality, never advising group members to stop taking medication or cancel the doctor's care. Small groups are not places to fantasize, exhibit self-punitive characteristics, or heap condemnation on people. S. Bruce Narramore notes:

> A third emotion related to guilt feelings and fears of punishment is what I call constructive sorrow. Paul writes of this in 2 Corinthians 7:9-10, where he reminds the Corinthians there is a difference between worldly sorrow that leads to death and godly sorrow that leads to righteousness. Constructive sorrow is a love-motivated emotion closely related to guilt feelings yet radically different. Whereas psychological guilt is a self-punitive process, constructive sorrow is a love-motivated desire to change that is rooted in concern for others. I believe a confusion of psychological guilt and constructive sorrow has often interfered with the church's efforts at promoting wholeness and health in the body of Christ (33).

Group leaders who have overcome a life-controlling problem should understand that their purpose is to facilitate learning and growth. They should not put themselves in a position as an expert, based on personal experience. A helper who has been affected by a family member's life-controlling problem should be aware of personal attitudes. Being intolerable to the values and lifestyles of others may prevent group members from receiving the help they need. Stephen P. Apthorp in his clergy handbook on alcohol and substance abuse notes:

> If a recovering alcoholic or recovering drug abuser is selected to be the "spark plug," it must be made clear to him that he is to be a facilitator of people, not a teacher or an expert witness by virtue of his personal experience. One of the fundamental characteristics of many a recovering person is the need to be in control and the need to control. . . . By the same token, selecting a parent whose child has been impaired by drug abuse may meet the requirements of enlisting a committed person, but in some cases the injury is such that it blocks the person's ability to tolerate others' attitudes, values, or lifestyles (33).

Communication Skills

Communication skills are extremely important in small-group interaction. Whether verbally or with silence, group members are always communicating in some manner. Effective communication requires active listening and having genuine concern for each group member. Since it is easy to develop poor patterns of interacting with people, communication skills require practice.

Open-ended questions help create discussion in the group. These types of questions cause the participants to have a better understanding of themselves. Repeating the content of the group member's message helps individuals know that they are being heard and that you are with them. When confronting is needed, carefronting skills should always be used.

As mentioned earlier, communications are enhanced by having people sit in a circle. Having the need for eye contact, all group participants should be able to see each other. Group members who sit across from each other tend to communicate better than those who sit next to each other. Group facilitators should sit across from each other and acknowledge all contributions to the group process. No one should ever be put down for a comment that is in error.

Group leaders should guard against the temptation to dominate the discussion. It is a common temptation to answer most of the questions, to be the *super* Christian, or to turn the group meeting into a platform for preaching. The leaders should give direction to the group process by starting the discussion then steering the conversation according to the curriculum being used. It is best to divert conversations on controversial subjects that may cause division among group members. Although the sharing of past experiences can be interesting and in some cases valuable, the focus of the small group should be on the present in the person's life. Since conversation on intellectual levels often results in surface discussion, it tends to kill personal sharing. There is a difference between what persons may *think* versus what they *feel*.

Handling excessive talkers in the group. There will be some people who tend to *overtalk* in the group or who may wish to show off their knowledge. Some may believe they have more knowledge than the facilitator (and they may); others may like the attention. There are certain communication skills that can be used to correct this situation. Questions and answers can be directed to individuals by name. Sitting next to the *overtalker* may help since the facilitator receives less eye contact than the other group members. This will cause the person to be away from the focus of attention and be less likely to respond.

The facilitators should analyze themselves to see if they are communicating clearly. If the group leaders are offensive, it is possible that the *overtalker* may see the need to take charge. It may be necessary to care-front the person privately. The *overtalker* may have leadership potential but needs to learn to be a better listener.

Handling nonparticipants. Some people are very timid or feel they do not have anything to contribute to the group. There are those who may also have reading difficulties. Group participants should be cared for with sensitivity (working within their comfort level). There are certain communication skills that can help increase their *comfort level.*

In all group sessions, the facilitators should remind participants that no one is expected to disclose if he or she does not want to talk. No one is forced to talk—everyone has the freedom to pass. Offering encouragement by gently directing to the shy persons questions that can be answered with ease and comfort will help them become active in the group discussion. These people should receive special attention before and after each group session. Group leaders may need to offer encouragement in private. Every answer they provide should be affirmed.

Phases in Group Life

Understanding the phases in group life is important for group facilitators. "Small groups go through stages as they begin, continue and end their life together. Just as an individual moves through stages in his life from infancy to old age, so groups, too, move through cycles" (Hestenes, 31). Although these phases may vary based on the personalities and experiences of the group members, certain phases are common with people who are dealing with life-controlling problems.

Trust building. In this initial phase, group participants are building trust in the group and in the leaders. Since group members may not know what to expect, they will be checking the integrity of the group experience. They will have concerns about confidentiality. They will usually discuss surface issues versus their real needs.

During this phase, the group facilitators' task is to develop an atmosphere of acceptance and love. In all go-arounds (a time of sharing for each group member) or exercises, they should first share themselves which will make group members more comfortable. Group members should be encouraged to share within their own *comfort level.* Participants will need help in seeing each group session as a part of the whole group life. They should be encouraged to be patient in their expectations. Although the entire group life involves trust building, the first three to four sessions will focus on trust.

Mutuality. In this second phase, emotional involvement deepens among group participants. As bonding among the participants develops, the group begins to take form. Individuals feel more free to express their feelings concerning their personal needs or concerns. Group members begin to share the leadership in the group process.

In this phase, the facilitators' task is to give more attention to the group process. The role begins to change as a leader to that of a facilitator. Being an active listener, the facilitator will need to clarify, reflect, and paraphrase responses from group participants. Since there may be those who will sidetrack the appropriate subject, the facilitators will tactfully need to keep the group on the subject.

Facilitators should also be aware of "unholy bonding." For example, if a person in the group is dealing with a sexual addiction, the leader should caution the person against sharing too much detail. Encourage the participant to say he or she is dealing with a personal sin or impurity. Further detailed sexual information could create lustful thinking among group members.

Affirmation. Group participants will begin to care-front each other with respect and sensitivity in this phase. They will support each other by pointing out the strengths of others and help with one another's struggles. Conflicts that surface should be viewed as a win-win versus a win-lose situation. There must be commitment to prayer throughout the group life because unresolved conflict can destroy a group. Group members should understand that commitment to each other means they should disagree agreeably.

Group participants will level within their *comfort zones* which will have significantly increased by this time. Seeing themselves more clearly with the help of others, they will begin to recognize the need to make changes that would please the Lord. Conversation will move from the casual to personal needs. Feeling less threatened, timid members will become more talkative. As the feeling of Christian community intensifies among the group members, participants will begin to value their time together.

Group facilitators need to help the participants focus on the Lord's work in their lives. "Let us fix our eyes on Jesus, the author and perfecter of our faith" (Hebrews 12:2). With the focus on the healing rather than the hurt, facilitators should encourage group members to support each other in love. Those who *overtalk* in the group should be tactfully discouraged by the helpers.

Accountability. In this final phase, group members learn to hold each other accountable. Although the group becomes very close, participants begin to develop more individual goals. As spiritual disciplines are developed, identity in Christ arises. They feel better about themselves. New ideas are offered, and some individuals may become *preachy.* If the group discontinues its meetings, the members will feel the pain of losing close friends. Termination may cause some to feel abandoned, or they may grieve over the loss of group acceptance and love.

In this phase the facilitators' task is to let go of the need to be the primary help. Participants should be encouraged to be committed to their local church. When the group terminates, leaders should offer encouragement and urge them to remain accountable to others in the body of Christ. Group facilitators should always encourage group participants to keep Christ as the center of their accountability.

Small Group Format

Each group session should consist of four phases covering a time frame of an hour and 15 minutes. The four phases are *Introduction, Self-Awareness, Spiritual Awareness,* and *Application.* There is a reason for each phase. The facilitators should always plan each session with this format in mind. Karl Menninger states:

The early Christian church cells were comprised of small groups of people who met regularly—often secretly. The order of worship was, first of all, self-disclosure and confession of sin, called exo-mologesis. This was followed by appropriate announcements of penance, pleas for forgiveness, and plans for making restitution. A final period of friendly fellowship (koinonia) closed the meeting (25).

Introduction. Begin with prayer. The facilitator may pray or may ask one of the group members to lead in prayer. After the prayer, a sharing question helps put the group at ease and makes them more comfortable in being a part of the discussion. The lead facilitator should respond to the sharing question first, followed by the co-facilitator. This causes the group members to feel safer in partici-pating in the exercise. After the facilitators have shared, the group members will share one after another around the circle. Always remind group members they are not expected to share if they do not wish to do so. The rule is that everyone works within his or her comfort level and is welcome to pass.

This is not the time for detailed conversation, so ask the mem-bers of the group to keep their comments brief. If a person is obvi-ously in pain during the exercise, the facilitator should interrupt the sharing and pray for the person in pain. After prayer, the exer-cise may resume.

Self-Awareness. After the sharing question, the facilitator will lead the group into the self-awareness phase which is a time to practice James 5:16, "Therefore confess your sins to each other and pray for each other so that you may be healed. The prayer of a righteous man is powerful and effective." It is important to stay on the subject matter. This is a time to focus on needs and healing, not to have a "martyr" or "pity party."

It is suggested in self-awareness that the facilitators ask the group members to share as they wish rather than going around the circle as in the introduction phase. This is because people are at various comfort levels, and they should not feel pressured to self-disclose if they are uncomfortable. As the group continues to meet, members will feel more and more comfortable in being a part of the discus-sion.

Remember, prayer is always in order. If a group member is hurting during this phase, stop and pray. One of the facilitators may lead in prayer or ask another group member to pray. This says to the group members that each member is important and that you care about each individual.

Spiritual Awareness. After the self-awareness phase, the facilitator will lead the group into the bible study time. Having briefly explained the topic, the facilitator should assign scriptures listed in the Facilitator's Guide to group members. When each scripture is called by the facilitator, the group member should read the verse(s). After the verses are read, give time for discussion.

Application. This part is actually a continuation of the spiritual awareness phase. Ask for volunteers to share their reflections on the question. The facilitators should emphasize the importance of the group members' applying biblical principles to their lives. Help for life-controlling problems begins with right thinking. The Bible says, "Be transformed by the renewing of your mind" (Romans 12:2). Obedience to the Word should follow with right behavior. Right feelings will follow right thinking and right behavior.

Small groups where Christ is the focus can bring wholeness in Christ to those who are struggling with life-controlling problems. Although it is true that believers can meet together and help each other overcome life-controlling problems, there should always be an emphasis on spiritual growth. To accomplish this, it is important for groups to have a planned curriculum that focuses on biblical principles. Without goals and facilitators to help implement these goals, the group will probably lack direction and may even develop a sickness mentality ("I am sick and will always be sick").

Help for an individual with a life-controlling problem begins with truthful thinking (thinking that yields to biblical principles). "Do not conform any longer to the pattern of this world, but be transformed by the renewing of your mind" (Romans 12:2). As people begin to change their behavior in obedience to God's Word, they will begin to experience right feelings. Although the development of a better understanding of one's self (self-awareness) is important, growth in Christ (spiritual awareness and application) should always remain the primary focus.

Three principles are provided in 1 John 3:18-20 which help us understand this process: principles of facts, faith, and feelings. First, the person should understand the *facts*. "Let us not love with words or tongue but with actions and in truth" (v18). Are our love and actions based on truth—on God's Word which is true (*see* Psalms 119:160)? Jesus Christ is actual, factual, and truthful (*see* Acts 1:3).

Second, a person's *faith* should be placed on the facts of God's Word. "We set our hearts at rest in his presence whenever our hearts condemn us. For God is greater than our hearts, and he knows everything" (1 John 3:19-20). Faith is accompanied by action (*see* James 2:17). To walk in faith, a person sets thoughts and feelings at rest in God's Word.

Third, a person's *feelings* will conform to the truth of God's Word. "If our hearts do not condemn us, we have confidence before God" (1 John 3:21). It is important to rest in God's promises when thoughts and feelings of condemnation come. (If an individual is not walking in truth, he or she should immediately get things worked out between himself or herself and God and get on with recovery.) *Feelings* are not the foundation of the Christian walk. Even after walking with the Lord for a long period of time, feelings may bring condemnation at which time a person will need to apply faith to the facts and then rest in God's presence. "But if we walk in the light, as he is in the light, we have fellowship with one another, and the blood of Jesus, his Son, purifies us from all sin" (1 John 1:7).

13

$\mathcal{M}$aking My Church a Biblical Model

An effective small group model for the local church must take into account the three tools of Satan that confront us: delusion, isolation, and hiding. Having 20 years of experience working with those who have a family member with a life-controlling problem, I have seen over and over again that the entire family is affected by the problem of the family member.

Families develop distorted thinking. Fathers, mothers, and other family members often create a survival system which perpetuates the systematic problem. Therefore, the struggle becomes a systems problem, not just an individual problem. This is especially true in light of today's addictive society. I have seen people whose commitment to Christ is without question make decisions about family matters that were no less than delusional. It is common for these people to pass on their delusional thinking to others in the body of Christ.

When problems with a family member intensifies, other family members may move into isolation and even try to hide instead of being honest with God and one another. Many fear the guilt of being seen as a failure or as a poor model for a Christian. After all, many think "these types of problems just don't happen to Christians." However, those who claim the most as far as their spirituality is concerned are often playing "mind games" with themselves and others. Regardless of a person's perceived spiritual stature, if that individual does not have accountability with fellow believers in his or her life, a fall is likely.

Small group ministry models for local churches vary to the extreme of recovery groups where there is no plan to incorporate those with life-controlling problems back into the body as a whole. Such labels perpetuate the problem. I have seen people who learn from the deviant behavior of others in an "all-alike problem group." These types of groups can reinforce preoccupation with the person's life-controlling problem. It may be necessary that such people have time together (alcoholics with alcoholics, sexually abused with the sexually abused, and so forth), but such groups cease to be effective if they are not integrated back into the cooperate body of believers.

On the other hand, the extreme of cell groups can develop into an atmosphere where the only spiritual event in the group meeting is praying before they eat their doughnuts. The value of cell groups, home groups, etc., is not in question; however, even in groups where there is strong biblical teaching, most people will continue to hide their struggles if there is not a platform for them to share their victories and struggles personally. Therefore, the perpetual problem continues, so many say, "We can't discuss such matters; this is work for the psychologist." Although no one should ever be pressured into sharing or getting their help in a church small group, what greater therapeutic community than the local church? It is my view the Church has erred more by giving up its role to the psychologist than the psychologist has by taking over the role from the Church. I have had Christian psychologists tell me that if the Church took its role as seriously as the *healing community*, their practice would greatly decrease.

It is not my purpose to knock counselors because I believe there will always be a need for one-on-one help for special cases; however, I must agree with Larry Crabb when he says that therapy belongs

back in the churches. In an interview with *Christianity Today*, Crabb
was asked about therapy in the church.

> What about the cell-and small-group movements that are currently
> taking root within the church? He said, "I see a lot of potential in
> these groups for building the kind of relationships in which people
> connect deeply and where the kind of eldering I'm talking about
> [godly men and women helping either in a discipleship or friend-
> ship capacity] could at least begin. If these groups can avoid being
> gatherings of either emotional gushers or rigid Bible students, they
> are a wonderful direction to go" (Miller, 17).

The most effective small groups are built on Bible-based common sense with Christ (not the leader, problems, or theories) as the
center. In an increasingly secular and dysfunctional society, there is
a need for relationship-based ministry that equips laypeople to help
each other deal with the struggles faced in daily living.

According to Carl George, "People must have the opportunity to
interact with each other, and in the process draw out a fuller appreciation for how they are accepted and loved and learned from . . ."
(69). A church that is prepared for the future must have a healthy
combination of corporate worship of God and small groups which
focus on relationships and felt needs. As discussed in Chapter 11,
the church at Thessalonica was a healthy example of the Word of
God, Spirit of God, and the people of God working together.

Turning Point: A Paradigm for Small Groups

Turning Point, although not a perfect model, has been an effective model for the local church since 1988 with over 1,400 churches currently involved. There are certain assumptions in this model:
(1) The Bible is the final authority for daily living, (2) the Holy
Spirit is working in this present day as teacher, counselor, and
guide, and (3) the community of believers under the lordship of
Jesus Christ is connected with each other and God. "From him
[Christ] the whole body, joined and held together by every sup-

porting ligament, grows and builds itself up in love, as each part does its work" (Ephesians 4:16).

This model emphasizes care that addresses the whole person. Paul helps us understand the uniqueness of the whole person: "May God himself, the God of peace, sanctify you through and through. May your whole spirit, soul and body be kept blameless at the coming of our Lord Jesus Christ" (1 Thessalonians 5:23). A person's body is weakened by life-controlling problems. The soul, which involves the mind, emotions, and will, loses touch with reality. As the mind and emotions become calloused and deluded, the spirit has difficulty relating with God. Although the soul and the spirit are thought of as being together (there are many scriptures to support this), each has distinct aspects that help us understand the inner being. Regarding these aspects, the writer of Hebrews states "For the word of God is living and active . . . it penetrates even to dividing soul and spirit" (4:12).

Humans make contact with the physical world through the body. This body which houses the soul and spirit is described as a human tent (*see* 2 Corinthians 5:1; 2 Peter 1:13-14). Causing much pain and suffering, life-controlling problems can be devastating to the human body. It comes as no surprise that the so-called sexual freedom (sex outside the boundaries of marriage, homosexuality, incest) is responsible for many sexually transmitted diseases that plague our society. With many life-controlling problems in the church at Corinth, Paul writes in 1 Corinthians 6:19-20: "Do you not know that your body is a temple of the Holy Spirit, who is in you, whom you have received from God? You are not your own; you were bought at a price. Therefore honor God with your body."

The soul (or self) consists of the mind, emotions, and will. Everything a person knows is stored in the mind (intellect). Perhaps the greatest struggles with a dependency is in the mind (deluded thinking). A person's emotions become entrapped causing behavior or feelings that bring enslavement. The person may lose the power to make choices or decisions. "The weapons we fight with are not the weapons of the world. On the contrary, they have divine power to demolish strongholds. We demolish arguments [imaginations] and every pretension that sets itself up against the knowledge of God, and we take captive every thought to make it obedient to Christ" (2 Corinthians 10:4-5). Paul also discusses the importance of having a renewed mind (*see* Romans 12:2; Ephesians 4:24; Colossians 3:10).

We make contact with God through the spirit (*see* John 4:23; Romans 8:16). God warned Adam in the Garden of Eden that he would die if he ate the forbidden fruit. When he ate of the tree, he died immediately spiritually (*see* Genesis 3) and later physically (*see* Genesis 5:5). We are spiritually dead (separated) without Christ; however, when we receive Christ as Savior, we are granted a new birth (*see* John 3). After the new birth, we are encouraged to "grow in the grace and knowledge of our Lord and Savior Jesus Christ" (2 Peter 3:18).

Since we have the potential of being in contact with the spiritual world, we can be influenced by forces that are not in agreement with Christ as the Son of God. The term *spirituality* is commonly used in circles unrelated to biblical truths, especially in the addiction field where there is an influx of New Age thinking. John warns in 1 John 4:1: "Dear friends, do not believe every spirit, but test the spirits to see whether they are from God, because many false prophets have gone out into the world."

God brings about change in us from the inside out. Our spirit must come in contact with God through Christ before there can be lasting change and fulfillment. Jesus says: "For from within, out of men's hearts, come evil thoughts, sexual immorality, theft, murder, adultery, greed, malice, deceit, lewdness, envy, slander, arrogance and folly. All these evils come from inside and make a man unclean" (Mark 7:21-23).

Small groups are the place for participants to take a close look at their lives through self-awareness. However, self-awareness is not enough; they need spiritual awareness which helps in their relationship with God. A balanced approach is important for them because God uses helpers to break the chains of life-controlling problems and deluded thinking. Frank Minirth and Paul Meier note:

God has given us the power of choice to live our lives to his glory or to ourselves and our own degradation. Choosing to live to his glory also means choosing to keep ourselves healthy in the physical, mental/emotional, and spiritual areas—body, soul, and spirit—of our lives. . . .

Body—knowing and taking care of our bodies, which are houses and temples for soul and spirit—ours and God's.
Soul—gaining insight into ourselves and growing in that insight.
Spirit—knowing the Lord and growing in him (97).

Organizational Mechanics

Having a local church model for people in this addictive society requires organization. To use laypeople effectively in ministry to those who are hurting or are affected by the hurting, the Church should provide a system and methodology that helps activate skills and concern. Along with interpersonal skills and a model, helpers will need various tools including training and curriculum to assist in activating the helping relationship.

Aspects of the Model

For the model to be effective, the pastor must offer his full support. The pastor (or pastoral staff) should endorse it in public, show up at early meetings, and offer encouragement to the effort and vision. Although the pastor may not be involved in the ministry activities, the model must stay under his *spiritual covering*. The minister oversees, a coordinator leads, and the core team manages. At full maturity, the core group oversees the model which has six components. [*Note:* This ministry model is presented in Turning Point Seminars. Curricula for *Insight Groups, Concerned Persons Groups*, and other related materials are available to churches after attendance at a seminar. For information, please write: Dr. Jimmy R. Lee, P. O. Box 22127, Chattanooga, TN 37422.]

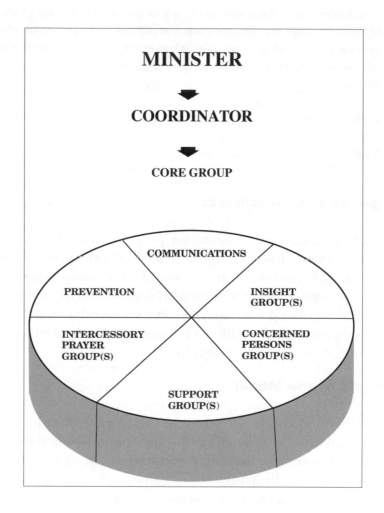

Figure 13-1: Local Church Model

The Core Team. The team consists of a group of laypeople in the local church who are trained to work with youth, adults, and families within the church and community. They are trained to work as a team to develop small groups which address the various aspects of living in an addictive society. As a team, the laypeople coordinate the program as a ministry to the local church body and to those in the community. The core team works cooperatively with the minister of the local church they serve. Each member of the core team should have a responsibility. The core team coordinator schedules the core group meetings and is the contact person for the minister. The coordinator serves as the representative of the core team. Some team members will serve as they are needed as leaders of small groups. Those who assist with communications will help present the goals of ministry to the church and community. Members who serve in the prevention component provide program and materials for Sunday school classes, youth groups, parents, and community.

Why is a core team needed? Because teamwork is important. Without the team approach, helpers are likely to become overburdened which can lead to burnout. It is impractical to think the ministerial staff alone can deal with the hurts and staggering needs most congregations face. In truth this work should be the responsibility of the entire local body of Christ. Churches in New Testament days were built on the assumption that believers would minister to each other. We can learn from this example and become people helpers. The core team should be respected by the congregation, trustworthy, and committed to Christ. They should be good role models, enthusiastic, positive, compassionate, and persistent.

Following the example of Christ's earthly ministry, there should be a team approach to ministry. "He appointed twelve—designating them apostles—that they might be with him and that he might send them out to preach" (Mark 3:14). There is strength in numbers. A team of people dividing the responsibilities of hand-in-hand helping is more efficient than one person who is trying to do everything. Helping people in a dysfunctional society is a big job—too big for one person in a local congregation.

The team approach to ministry benefits not only those who are being helped but also those who are doing the helping. Persons serving Christ on a core team will experience the joy of helping others as well as the encouragement and support of fellow team members. What a comfort to know that others are there to help with tough problems, to encourage you to be faithful to your calling, and to pray for you specifically.

To meet the varied and specific responsibilities of the core team, look for persons with these characteristics:

The core team coordinator must be an organizer and delegator. This person loves to organize people and projects and is probably a list maker. A delegator knows when to ask for help and whom to ask.

The prevention coordinator must be an idea person and a resource person. This person is full of suggestions for everything from family Christmas gifts to raising funds for the homeless. A resource person loves the library and takes joy in matching a person with a helpful book.

The intercessory prayer coordinator must be a faithful prayer warrior. This person does not just talk about prayer but prays daily because he or she believes prayer makes a difference.

The communications coordinator must be a good communicator. This is someone who does not mind standing in front of others and giving a short, motivating announcement.

Insight Group, Concerned Persons, and Support Group facilitators must have these characteristics: a vibrant spiritual life, a servant's heart, a positive attitude, a consistent track record, and a listening ear.

The core team should meet at least once every two weeks. Having an agenda carefully prepared by the coordinator helps to keep the meetings on target. The agenda should include a word of encouragement and a passage of scripture. Other items should include a progress report from each small group, discussion about new groups, and a report from those responsible for prevention. The meeting is a time to pray for specific needs and give support to each other. Needing teamwork and support, the core team should plan fun activities together. A total of 10-15 core team members is sufficient; however, a very large church may need 30-40 helpers or even multiple core teams.

The Turning Point model places an emphasis on training and curriculum for small groups in three main areas: (1) focused discipleship (special needs such as drug addictions, alcoholism, eating disorders, sexual addictions, etc.), (2) general discipleship that focuses on felt needs, and (3) friend-to-friend evangelism.

Insight Group. We recommend the *Insight Group* as the entry group for all church attendees because it helps people develop a better understanding of themselves and focuses on discovering the path to Christian character. Showing pitfalls that we may be unaware of, the *Insight Group* examines the hindering aspects of living in an addictive society. It also helps people understand each other and often surfaces problems before they become life-controlling. The Apostle Paul says:

> Remember that some men's sins are obvious, and are equally obviously bringing them to judgment. The sins of other men are not apparent, but are dogging them, nevertheless, under the surface. Similarly some virtues are plain to see, while others, though not at all conspicuous, will eventually become known(1 Timothy 5:24-25, PHILIPS).

The *Insight Group* helps people move into deeper Christian growth and meaningful relationships in subsequent small group interaction.

Insight Group Overview. Following is an overview of all nine sessions which shows how each one fits into the overall Insight Group purpose:

Session One: Orientation. This is the introduction session of the *Insight Group.* Facilitators will first introduce themselves and then ask the same from the participants. This session explains the Insight Group purpose, the meeting format, and the ground rules for the group.

An overview of the eight objectives (*faith, goodness, knowledge, self-control, perseverance, godliness, brotherly kindness,* and *love*) from 2 Peter 1:3-11 is presented. Stress that the exercise of one objective develops the next one. (For example: The exercise of faith in Christ develops goodness, the exercise of goodness develops knowledge, etc.). The great promises in 2 Peter 1:3-4 are emphasized.

Session Two: Trust. Sharing biographical data about such subjects as family, friends, school, work, and others helps build trust within the group. Beginning with the facilitators, this is a "get-to-know-you" session.

The spiritual awareness segment shifts the emphasis to the first of eight objectives or qualities found in 2 Peter 1:5—*faith* in Jesus Christ. Faith in Christ is the foundation of our Christian life, and the highest trust should be placed in Him because He is trustworthy.

Session Three: The Trap. The facilitators introduce the stages of life-controlling problems in this session. Participants are given the opportunity to take a look at their lives as they relate to the trap which is presented in four steps or stages.

The spiritual awareness focus is on the second objective: *goodness* (virtue, moral excellence, and resolution). The emphasis in this session is placed on making a commitment to moral excellence. Participants should see that the exercise of our faith in Christ provides the energy we need to follow through on our commitment to moral excellence and to experience a life free of mastering problems.

Session Four: Feelings. In this session the Johari Window is used as an object lesson to show how our true feelings can be hidden from us (especially as we continue to practice a mastering problem), yet those feelings can be seen by others. A person who lives with hidden feelings is living in delusion. Participants are given an opportunity to share one of six feelings which are listed.

Beginning with the spiritual awareness lead-in question, the emphasis is placed on the third objective: *knowledge.* As we exercise goodness and a commitment to moral excellence, we grow in knowledge and begin to live in light of who we are in Christ and not on the basis of feelings.

Session Five: Defenses and Isolation. This discussion points out how defenses are often used to build a wall around our life-controlling problems. This wall is built to protect us from the truth. Participants are given an opportunity to take a look at their own defenses in a nonthreatening way. Note that it is important that the walls (or defenses) in each group member's life come down brick by brick instead of by the bulldozer approach.

The spiritual awareness segment focuses on the fourth objective (or quality) found in 2 Peter 1: *self-control.* The exercise of the knowledge of Christ in our lives develops self-control. Mastery over physical appetites helps us deal with the lies (deceptive defenses) that surround us.

Session Six: Symptoms. This session brings to the attention of participants the symptoms that often accompany life-controlling problems. The facilitators should lead the discussion on the noticeable progression of these symptoms. Having discussed denial, delusions, and feelings in previous sessions, participants may now see themselves more clearly and relate with one or more of these signs.

Beginning with the spiritual awareness lead-in, the emphasis begins to focus on the fifth objective: *perseverance.* This is a challenge to persevere and work through all the symptoms by being honest with God and one another. Facilitators should point out that as the participants practice self-control, God will help them "hang in there" and develop the perseverance that will keep them from falling back into the old patterns of their life-controlling problems.

Session Seven: Ministry to One Another. Beginning with this session, participants will be given an opportunity to share one-by-one their progress—or lack of progress—as a member of this group. Peer ministry will continue with sessions eight and nine, so facilitators should limit participants receiving peer ministry in this session to one-third of the group. Through ministry to each other, group members will provide loving, caring, and constructive feedback to each person as he or she shares his or her life as a part of this group.

Beginning with the spiritual awareness lead-in, the emphasis is placed on the sixth objective: *godliness.* As a person practices perseverance, a lifestyle that reflects godliness is developed. Facilitators should note that as group members practice peer care, they can encourage one another to be godly.

Session Eight: Ministry to One Another Continues. This is a continuation of session seven as another third of the participants, one-by-one, are given an opportunity to receive peer ministry from the group. Through the peer ministry, group members will provide loving, caring, and constructive feedback to each person as he or she shares his or her life as a part of this group.

The spiritual awareness time focuses on the seventh objective: *brotherly kindness.* As a person practices godliness, it is natural that his or her attitudes and actions toward others would be more like God's, thus brotherly kindness is developed. Facilitators should emphasize that peer ministry, as we express love and care for each other, is an aspect of brotherly kindness.

Session Nine: Ministry to One Another Concludes. This session continues the peer ministry as the remaining group members are given an opportunity to receive loving, caring, and constructive feedback from the group.

Beginning with the spiritual awareness lead-in question, the focus is on the eighth objective: *love.* As a person exercises brotherly kindness, Christian love is developed. Facilitators should point out that the peer ministry of these last three sessions is a practical example of how we can show love to our peers because of the love God has shown to us.

Everyone in the church will benefit from the *Insight Group.* It is also effective for unbelievers brought into the group by a friend who is a believer. The *Insight Group* pictures life-controlling problems as a downward spiral that pulls a person deeper and deeper and then presents the character qualities found in 2 Peter 1:3-11 as a ladder that helps us climb out of the deep hole of a life-controlling problem. The eight qualities are: faith, goodness, knowledge, self-control, perseverance, godliness, brotherly kindness, and love. As we exercise one, the next one develops. For example, as we exercise faith in Christ, we develop goodness; as we exercise goodness, we develop knowledge, and so forth.

This group helps to enhance people's understanding of each other and how this relates to everyday practical problems. It helps prepare people for more meaningful relationships in subsequent small groups such as home groups, cells, and Sunday school classes. It surfaces people for help who may otherwise never seek help.

The *Insight Group* helps break down the segregation of people in churches by turning "those people" and "our kind of people" into just "us." This is an effective entry group for small groups.

Concerned Persons Group. There are three basic types of life-controlling problems: substances, behaviors, and relationships. This small group is primarily for those who want to help someone close to them who is enslaved by a stronghold. This group is also for people who are suffering the consequences of a loved one's life-controlling problem. Quite often these participants are struggling with very sensitive and emotional issues and need compassion and comfort. "Praise be to the God and Father of our Lord Jesus Christ, the Father of compassion and the God of all comfort, who comforts us in all our troubles, so that we can comfort those in any trouble with the comfort we ourselves have received from God" (2 Corinthians 1:3-4).

The purpose of this group is to encourage and strengthen each group member in God's love. Group facilitators should exhibit love, honesty, and respect without being judgmental. All *Concerned Persons Group* members should complete the *Insight Group* as a prerequisite to this group as it helps to prepare them for this group. Even though they may want to learn how to help as a concerned person, participation in an *Insight Group* helps them begin the process by looking at themselves first. This group should meet once each week for an hour and 15 minutes over a period of nine weeks. Group facilitators should follow the small group format (*see* pages 175-176) in applying the curriculum content.

Understanding the Times

Concerned Persons Group Overview. Following is an overview of all nine sessions which shows how each one fits into the overall Concerned Persons Group purpose:

Session One: Comfort During this first meeting of the Concerned Persons Group, facilitators introduce themselves and give group members an opportunity to meet each other. Group members learn about the purpose of the Concerned Persons Group and the format each session will follow. Facilitators also explain the ground rules for the group.

The spiritual awareness segment focuses on the subject of *comfort*. A bible study based on 2 Corinthians 1:3-8 introduces "the God of all comfort and the Father of compassion." The group will discuss the nature of God's comfort—how we can experience it and how we can share that comfort with others in their need.

Session Two: Hope. Pressure, frustration, and the resulting overload are discussed in session two. Group members are given an opportunity to talk about the kinds of pressure and overload they are experiencing in their role as concerned persons.

Feelings of frustration and hopelessness are common among concerned persons because of their inability to "fix" their loved one's problem, so it is appropriate that the bible study in this session looks at the source of true *hope*. Hope is defined as "an attitude of confident expectation of something good." This hope is built on who God is, our confidence in His Word, and the power of prayer.

Session Three: Codependency. The characteristics and dangers of codependent relationships are the focus of the self-awareness segment. Participants will look at their own relationships as concerned persons and how they can set healthy personal boundaries.

Beginning with the spiritual awareness lead-in, codependency is contrasted with *interdependency*. Codependence and independence are both out of balance, but the bible study examines the balanced and God-ordained interdependence of believers within the body of Christ.

Session Four: Feelings and Defenses. Group members will discuss the importance of recognizing their real feelings and expressing them appropriately. The use of I-messages rather than You-messages is an effective communication skill taught in this session.

The bible study time centers on the subject of *feelings*, especially the feelings Christ experienced in His time on earth. It is important for group members to understand that Christ understands our feelings and our weaknesses and is in Heaven making intercession for us.

Session Five: Letting Go and Letting God. This session draws attention to the emotional stages commonly experienced by the family and close friends of an addicted or dependent individual. These stages closely parallel the grief process that a dying person and his or her loved ones go through. Participants are encouraged to examine their relationships for signs of enabling behavior.

The spiritual awareness segment emphasizes the need to recognize our *powerlessness* to fix what is wrong in a loved one's life. Group members are encouraged to give their concerns for their troubled loved ones to God and then let Him work in that life.

Session Six: Care-fronting. Care-fronting is a valuable communication tool to reach through the defenses and denial of loved ones and allow them to hear the truth in a nonthreatening way. Care-fronting brings together the two ideas of caring and confrontation. Specific guidelines for effective care-fronting are discussed.

In the spiritual awareness segment, the biblical basis for *caring confrontation* is drawn from the life of Jesus as well as the instruction to believers found in Ephesians 4:15 to speak the truth in love. Group members discuss the relationship between their role as care-fronters and the convicting work of the Holy Spirit.

Session Seven: Ministry to One Another. In this session participants, one-by-one, are given an opportunity to share their progress or lack of progress as a member of this group. Peer ministry will continue with sessions eight and nine, so facilitators should limit participants receiving peer ministry in this session to three (or the appropriate number) so each one will have an opportunity to share in sessions seven through nine. Through ministry to each other, group members will provide loving, caring, and constructive feedback to each person as he or she shares his or her life as a part of this group.

Beginning with the spiritual awareness lead-in, the emphasis moves to the subject of the *healing*—emotional, spiritual, social, and even physical—that is often needed in the life of a concerned person. The ministry of others, open communication with God through prayer, and forgiveness—of our loved ones and of ourselves—are all a part of the healing process.

Session Eight: Ministry to One Another Continues. This is a continuation of session seven as participants, one-by-one, are given an opportunity to receive peer ministry from the group. Through the peer ministry, group members will provide loving, caring, and constructive feedback to each person as he or she shares his or her life as a part of this group.

The spiritual awareness time focuses on the importance of *setting goals* for the future. The Apostle Paul's picture of himself as being in a race—pressing on for the prize—is applied to the circumstances of a concerned person. This bible study stresses the importance of moving past the memories that would lead to a defeated attitude and moving ahead to become all God wants us to be.

Session Nine: Ministry to One Another Concludes. This session continues the peer ministry as the remaining group members are given an opportunity to receive loving, caring, and constructive feedback from the group.

Beginning with the spiritual awareness lead-in question, the focus of this session moves to the importance of *renewing our minds* and beginning to think God's way. It is common for concerned persons to have a problem in the area of self-worth and value. This study helps group members to see themselves as God sees them—

in Christ—forgiven, His workmanship, heaven-bound, free from accusation, and more. This session concludes with an opportunity for group members to consider and share how their personal focus has changed over the nine weeks of Concerned Persons Group.

The *Concerned Persons Group* helps those who want to help someone close to them. It helps those who are suffering the consequences of a loved one's life-controlling problem; for example, a husband or wife with an alcoholic or addicted spouse or the parents of a troubled child. The group helps to provide a better understanding of how a life-controlling problem affects the entire family.

It contains important self-awareness principles and timely biblical principles aimed at offering encouragement and strength in God's love. The Concerned Persons Group is designed for the many people who have a current or past relationship with a person who has a life-controlling problem. The group emphasizes the need we all have for each other and helps people focus on Christ rather than on the problem. It is effective in home groups, support groups, recovery groups, and cell groups.

New members should not be added to the *Insight* or *Concerned Persons Group* after the second meeting. When the group is interrupted with new members, the progress of the group is slowed, and the new member may not feel a part of the group. To handle the continuing influx of new members, *Insight* and *Concerned Persons* groups should be started at staggered times. For example, one *Insight Group* and *Concerned Persons Group* could start today. The next group would begin in three or four weeks. People wanting to join a group between start-up times can be assigned to a *Support Group* (topical study) until the next group starts.

Support Group. The Support Group is for participants who desire continued help, having already been through the *Insight Group* and *Concerned Persons Group*. With the experience of having been through the *Insight* and *Concerned Persons* groups, participants will understand the self-awareness and spiritual awareness phases. Facilitators may select the appropriate curriculum for the *Support*

Group. Choices may include a Christ-centered twelve-step program, Sunday school curriculum, or a specialized study for the spiritual awareness. See page 197.

Friend-to-friend Evangelism. What does it mean to reach out? We know that today an invitation to church is often going to fall on deaf ears, but an invitation to a small group where you might learn how to avoid life-controlling struggles or how to overcome them—that's a different story. Paul describes friend-to-friend evangelism in 1 Thessalonians 2:8: "We loved you so much that we were delighted to share with you not only the gospel of God but our lives as well, because you had become so dear to us."

Small groups can level the playing field because they do not label people or separate the believer from the unbeliever. It is based on some common ground that says all of us struggle with a life-controlling problem to some degree. Some of us may be in the early stages of a life-controlling problem; others of us are in more advanced stages.

Consider the impact of a believer's inviting an unbeliever to attend a felt-need small group. The believer may be highly motivated to see his friend come to Christ, but he is taking on a servant role and humbling himself to say, "I'm no different or better than you. Let's discover together how to avoid or overcome a life-controlling problem."

Having a local church model that provides principles for reaching out to those who are hurting can be an effective evangelism tool. A congregation that has an air of superiority or makes a person feel inferior will not be effective. The church that reaches out with acceptance, although with firm love, will stand tall in the community. Their caring will present them with the right to be heard. "If I speak in the tongues of men and of angels, but have not love, I am only a resounding gong or a clanging cymbal" (1 Corinthians 13:1).

After the church has established a model for ministering to the hurting, it can consider referrals from court systems, social agencies, places of employment, and school counselors. Ministries can be started on high school and college campuses with the local church model; however, it is important to understand the position of school officials and board policies. The best approach may be from a serving position versus one's rights to be on campus. A low-key approach with consistency is one way to let our light shine: "Let your light shine before men, that they may see your good deeds and praise your Father in heaven" (Matthew 5:16).

Since most prisoners are incarcerated because of a crime committed as a result of an addiction, a felt need can be met in jails and prisons. With each person helped, the door of ministry is opened up to reach entire families. This type of ministry touches families where they really live. "Jesus said, 'It is not the healthy who need a doctor, but the sick'" (Matthew 9:12). Since 15 million Americans are meeting weekly in various kinds of support groups (according to Leerhsen and Namuth, *Newsweek*, February 5, 1990), Christ-centered support groups can be a tremendous tool for evangelism.

According to J. David Schmidt, a local church consultant:

Churches in North America may continue to grow on biological and transfer growth but without a doubt the number-one need of the local church in this country is to discover how to effectively penetrate secular society with the gospel, to provide doors of entry into the church for the seeker (Lee, 1991, 1).

Figure 13-2: Flow Chart

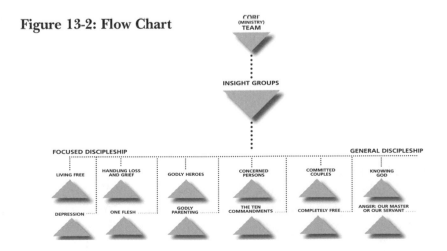

Intercessory Prayer Group. This group meets weekly to pray specifically for the minister, congregation, and those involved in the helping ministry. Helping people with life-controlling problems is a spiritual warfare. "For our struggle is not against flesh and blood, but against the rulers, against the authorities, against the powers of this dark world and against the spiritual forces of evil in the heavenly realms" (Ephesians 6:12).   Charles Stanley in his work on prayer states:

> It is time we quit struggling against flesh and blood and deal with the real enemy. We have only one weapon. It is not preaching, teaching, singing, or organizing; it is the Word of God brought against Satan's lies through prayer. Our prayers build the Kingdom of God and destroy the Kingdom of Satan(120).

Prevention. Those core team members involved in prevention serve as a resource for the various ministries of the church. Their primary focus is to provide healthy alternatives based on biblical principles of living for youth and adults. For example, programs can be presented on how to say no to substances and behaviors that may enslave a person. "For the grace of God that brings salvation has appeared to all men. It teaches us to say 'No' to ungodliness and worldly passions, and to live self-controlled, upright and godly lives in this present age" (Titus 2:11-12). The primary institution to deal with the prevention of drugs, AIDS, abortions, and premarital sex is the family and the local church, not the schools.

Communications. The core team members involved in communications present the goals of the helping ministry to the church and the community. They inform the congregation when and where small groups will meet. They also assist group members in signing up for the appropriate group. Announcements on a church bulletin board and in church newsletters can be effective in getting the *word out.* Television and radio advertisements are useful in getting the ministry known among the community. Visits to social agencies, school counselors, and judges can result in referrals to the local church helping ministry. Printed materials that describe the ministry should be given to interested agencies. Announcements and advertising helps to inform people; however, the personal invitation remains the best form of communication.

The Legal Aspects. With the heightened litigation mood, churches should take certain precautions in their ministry to people in this addictive society. Helpers should focus on spiritual versus psychological care. From a clearly written statement, participants should know what they can expect in small group activities. The statement should explain that the approach is primarily spiritual and biblical rather than psychological or physiological. For example:

> *Please understand that this ministry is not a substitute for medical or psychological care. We never advise anyone to stop taking medication or cancel their doctor's care.*
>
> *We give our time, compassion, and love solely as caring people who want to be channels of Christ's love to those who are hurting and desire wholeness in Christ. As noncredentialed persons, we promise no professional psychological expertise.*

Although it may not be intentional, group facilitators should never deceive participants with misleading claims concerning a leader or the group's ability to solve a participant's problem. The focus should always remain on Christ and biblical principles. Misleading claims can be avoided by following a set curriculum for each session. Having two facilitators reduces the possibility of one leader's becoming the *spiritual or psychological guru.*

Confidentiality should be explained during the orientation session of the group life. What is discussed in the group will not be mentioned outside the group. During the discussion regarding confidentiality, the facilitators should discuss the ground rules of confidentiality in that confidentiality will be broken if people are a danger to themselves or to others (i.e., the revealing of suicidal tendencies or the reporting of child abuse). Second, the pastor has privilege to the confidentiality of the group. As the spiritual leader of the congregation, he should have privilege to this information if he so desires or the facilitators deem it helpful.

Group leaders should beware of their limitations. Some participants may need the care of professional Christian counselors. There are certain elements facilitators can use as indicators. If a person has a long history of firmly rooted problems or if a person shows signs of repressed memories, he or she may need professional care. Working with those who have strong tendencies toward self-punishment and condemnation can be difficult. Some may not have clearly defined problems, or they may be tormented with deep depression. A person in the group who is struggling with an addiction and shows no signs of abstinence (even temporary abstinence) may need the care of a treatment program. Group facilitators should, in consultation with their minister, offer various referral options from which participants may choose.

Getting Started

The minister should select a coordinator and core team to start the Turning Point model. In larger churches there may be a need for more than one core team to implement this ministry. Almost every church has a group interested in this type of ministry. The group should receive specific training. After the training, the core team should participate in an *Insight Group* together before the members actually start the functions of the team. Attending the *Insight Group* is important for three reasons: (1) Helpers should be aware of their own spiritual and emotional needs, (2) attending the Insight Group sends an important message to the congregation: *This ministry is for everyone*, and (3) helpers receive on-the-job training.

An effective ministry that will help people at all phases of life-controlling problems should be focused toward the mainstream of the congregation. As mentioned previously, in the typical evangelical congregation 20 percent of the people do most of the work and are usually committed regardless of circumstances. Another 20 percent struggle with immense problems that affect their relationship with God and their commitment to the local church body. The remaining 60 percent are the mainstream. Some are being affected by life-controlling problems; however, they do not see them as problems. Others may be concerned about a life-controlling problem, but they deny its existence to others.

The deniers in the mainstream segment of the church are more likely to get involved since they are not labeled as being addicted, dependent, or sick. The 20 percent who do most of the work will likely be involved if the ministry is promoted as discipleship, and many of the 20 percent who are struggling will also participate because their problems are already at a mastering phase.

To prevent labeling, the Insight Group which is the entry group for all participants in the small-group process deals with addiction in generic terms. No specific addiction is highlighted because the dynamics of most dependencies are the same regardless of the type (drugs, alcohol, sex, gambling, eating disorders, and so forth). This helps the church develop a more acceptable and sensitive environment for those who may not want to be identified as having a problem—even though they may. This approach helps to avoid the stigma of the ministry's being only for "sick" people since it targets everyone in the church.

Using this approach should assist the local church body in dealing with traditional church attitudes that create resistance toward helping the hurting. Certain myths contribute to resistance. One of the greatest myths concerns the term *life-controlling problem*. To some people, this description conjures up extreme images: an alcoholic passed out on the floor after a drinking binge, a heroin junkie scrambling for another fix, or a nymphomaniac hopping from bed to bed. To some people, a life-controlling problem is just another name for addiction.

These people may not recognize the fact that life-controlling problems include such general life areas as unhealthy relationships and perfectionism. They may not understand how the family is affected by a family member's life-controlling problem.

Many difficulties that surface in the local church may find their root in a life-controlling problem. To view this ministry model as a program for addicts is to lose sight of the wide-reaching scope of the ministry and potential ministry participants.

After participants have completed the *Insight Group*, they should participate in a *Concerned Person's Group*. Since most people have a concern about a friend or loved one's problem or are affected by the consequences of a significant other's behavior, the *Concerned Person's Group* will provide a greater awareness and support for them. After completing the *Concerned Person's Group*, they may need continued participation in an ongoing support group that address-es a specific need. To keep the momentum going in your church, this model is designed to be—and works much more effectively as— a process, not a disjointed, erratic series of small group studies. Three elements are necessary for implementing a "process" mind-set in the ministry: *a master plan, continuous new leadership training,* and *communication.*

Before a ministry can have a "process" mind-set, it must have a complete, prayerful assessment of *where it wants to go.* A master plan is needed. The plan must be in tune with the specifics of the min-istry. Factors such as the number of ministry participants, the num-ber of available leaders, and calendar schedule must be considered.

The plan should be comprehensive and detailed. In drawing it up, ministry leaders should consider every question that might be asked about the ministry:

"What if a leader is unable to be at a meeting?"

"How and when will we train new leaders?"

"How will we promote the ministry?"

"What options will group members have when they complete a small group study?"

Not only should the plan be comprehensive and detailed, but it should also be flexible. It is impossible to foresee everything that might occur within the ministry. Just because something is planned does not mean it will occur, and just because something is planned does not mean it will occur as expected. Provisions and alternatives should be built into the plan to account for the natural processes of turnover and attrition. By the same token, flexibility in the plan will allow ministry leaders the chance to take advantage of opportuni-ties that arise.

One of the obvious by-products of a *process* mentality is ministry growth, and as more and more people join the ministry, the need for leaders increases. Therefore, a process mentality is impossible without continuous, new leadership training. Leaders of the ministry should always be on the lookout for potential leaders. Every ministry participant should be assumed to be a potential leader until proven otherwise. Once a viable leadership candidate is identified, that person should be encouraged and trained.

If this model of ministry is to be viewed as a "process," it must be *communicated* as such. Not only must the master plan be created, but it must also be communicated to the congregation. People interested in the ministry must recognize from the beginning that it is not a onetime occurrence. Promotion can also be used to relate information to those interested in becoming leaders. A steady flow of such information is bound to yield dividends.

A master plan, continuous new leadership training, and communication—when used effectively together—can transform a disjointed, stop-and-start ministry into a *process.*

Initial Promotion

The best way to promote this type of ministry in the church initially is simply by word of mouth. The core team coordinator and the pastor should contact people they think would be interested in being a part of the core team. A pulpit announcement may be appropriate.

Once the core team is established and ready to launch Insight Groups, the promotional needs will change. Although word of mouth will continue to be the best advertisement, following are suggestions on how to promote the ministry model throughout the congregation:

An announcement from the pulpit:

In an increasingly secular and dysfunctional society, we see more and more the need for relationship-based ministry so that we can help each other deal with struggles faced in daily living. According to Carl George, a recognized church growth author, "People must have the opportunity to interact with each other and, in the process, draw out a fuller appreciation for how they are accepted by and are loved by and learn from . . . each other." A church needs a healthy combination of corporate worship of God and small groups which focus on relationships and felt needs.

We see the need for small groups in three main areas:

1. *Focused discipleship (special needs such as drug addictions, alcoholism, eating disorders, sexual addictions, etc.)*
2. *General discipleship that focuses on felt needs*
3. *Friend-to friend evangelism*

We recommend the Insight Group as the entry group for all in the church because it helps us develop a better understanding of ourselves and focuses on discovering the path to Christian character.

We are in the process of launching a ministry that helps us practice the one another care which is often mentioned in the New Testament. This ministry, Turning Point, relates the power of Scripture to where people are and gives them practical handles for release from their problems. If the church is a hospital, think of Turning Point as the support unit.

*Notice the Turning Point insert in your bulletin. Turning Point is **not** just for those struggling with a life-controlling problem themselves but for anyone wanting more insight into life-controlling problems—how they can be prevented and how the truths of Scripture relate.*

Join us (date, time, and location) for a brief meeting that will answer all your questions about this ministry.

Commitment Encouraged

Since there can be various obstacles, there must be a high level of commitment from the core team. Some people may resist the ministry because of personal biases. The comments may range from "ain't it a shame nothing can be done" to "only professionals can do this kind of ministry." To be successful, the ministry will need the same priority given to other important ministries of the church.

Persistence Required

It may take some time to start a helping ministry for people with life-controlling problems since some people in the congregation may view the ministry as another fad. Persistence will help build credibility. Some people will take the "wait and see" approach. They may need support, but it may take time to gain their confidence so they will seek out support. The ministry must be worked as a marathon race versus a sprint. Helpers will burn out if they do not pace themselves. As people see the consistency of the ministry, more individuals will come for help. "If properly developed, it is my perhaps optimistic but I think realistic hope that every counseling need (except ones which involve organic problems) would be met within the church community" (Crabb, 165).

Summary

Life-controlling problems hidden *behind our Sunday smiles* can cause great harm to our relationships with God and others. This ministry must come in the front door of the church and be viewed as available for everyone. People should not be labeled as addicts or with some other description that may cause them to feel isolated from the congregation. Labels may cause people to feel inferior or contribute to a sense of hopelessness. Gary Sweeten in his work on the eight core conditions of helping states:

One of the keys to healing mental illness is to not label persons with diagnostic labels. A World Health Organization study found that in those countries that placed such labels on persons struggling with emotional stability, the recidivism rate (getting sick again) was much higher than in those countries where people were not labeled (62).

Although labels can be valuable to summarize information, we should be careful not to judge or limit people with labels. Pinning labels on people may contribute to the segregation of the body of Christ or pride in the problem: "I am chemically dependent, and no one in this church can help me." Labels such as "mid-life crisis" and "youth must go through a rebellious stage" [he must sow his wild oats] are often used to excuse or enforce negative behaviors.

Having a *sincere smile* or seemingly *having it together* does not mean a person is not struggling with a life-controlling problem. Ministry to these people and those who are in obvious pain or sorrow is Jesus at work. "When did we see you a stranger and invite you in, or needing clothes and clothe you? When did we see you sick or in prison and go to visit you? The King will reply, 'I tell you the truth, whatever you did for one of the least of these brothers of mine, you did for me' " (Matthew 25:38-40).

14

Committed to Making a Difference

Commitment is a word that is downplayed by this addictive society. Lack of commitment is seen in high divorce rates, lack of ethical conduct, breakdown of the family, and the list goes on and on. Conditional attachment has replaced commitment in most relationships. A person committed to God, family, and church will stand above this crowded dysfunctional society.

Daniel is a biblical character who is an example of commitment for the present mind-set—conditional attachment. Daniel and his three friends, Shadrach, Meshach and Abednego, were among those taken captive to Babylon the year Nebuchadnezzar besieged Jerusalem. Being well-qualified, they were among those chosen to serve in the king's palace. This meant they would receive the finest of training and eat from the king's table. They would attend the king's college for three years and then enter the king's service.

Being in the king's college meant they would be exposed to the glamour and wealth of Babylon. They were in an enticing position to forsake their religion and pursue worldly success. With their

freedom gone and their temple destroyed, their faith in Almighty
God would be tested. Daniel, a sixteen-year-old teenager, and his
three Hebrew friends were given new names, but their faith in God
remained the same. There are characteristics in Daniel's life that
will work for us in this present day "conditional attachment" environment.

Committed to his convictions. Daniel was committed to his convictions. "Daniel resolved not to defile himself with the royal food and
wine" (Daniel 1:8). Because the food did not meet the require-
ments of the Mosaic law, Daniel said no to the food and wine which
had been offered to idols as was the custom in Babylon. Daniel said
no to Nebuchadnezzar and yes to God. There was no wavering or
rationalizing on his part. He was quick in making up his mind—no
indecision. James writes, "But when he asks, he must believe and
not doubt, because he who doubts is like a wave of the sea, blown
and tossed by the wind. That man should not think he will receive
anything from the Lord; he is a double-minded mind, unstable in
all he does"(James 1:6-8).

Daniel was familiar with the "just say no club" long before we
were. This teenager was not influenced by hypocritical athletes and
movie stars to say "no"; he was motivated on the inside by God to
stay true to his convictions. The grace of God teaches us to say "no."
Paul writes, "For the grace of God that brings salvation has
appeared to all men. It teaches us to say 'No' to ungodliness and
worldly passions, and to live self-controlled, upright and godly lives
in this present age" (Titus 2:11-12).

Committed to building relationships. "He asked the chief official for
permission not to defile himself this way" (Daniel 1:8). Instead of
demanding his way or arrogantly condemning others, Daniel asked
permission not to partake of the royal food and wine. Three times
he is referred to as being "highly esteemed" (9:23; 10:11, 19). It is
not without significance that Daniel spoke "with wisdom and tact"
(2:14).

Daniel was respected by others because he took time to build
relationships. It takes time to build one another relationships. I
have difficulty picturing Daniel marching with a placard in his

hand saying, "Just say no to Nebuchadnezzar." His godly attitude toward building relationships earned him the right to be heard. Godly actions speak louder than marches for our favorite cause or bumper stickers which have been described as America's pulpit above the tail pipe. Anybody can speak from a bumper sticker. Daniel's pulpit was building relationships without compromising his values.

Commitment brought him in favor with the official. "Now God had caused the official to show favor and sympathy to Daniel" (Daniel 1:9). The chief official was concerned about the request to change the diet. He said, "Why should he [the king] see you looking worse than the other young men your age? The king would then have my head because of you" (1:10). The chief official agreed to the alternative diet even though it could mean the loss of his life because God had given Daniel favor in the eyes of the chief official. "For the eyes of the LORD range throughout the earth to strengthen those whose hearts are fully committed to him" (2 Chronicles 16:9).

His commitment influenced others. Daniel was an influence on Shadrach, Meshach, and Abednego. He built positive relationships with these companions. It seems these young men felt comfortable with Daniel's leadership since he spoke to the guard for them. "Daniel then said to the guard whom the chief official had appointed over Daniel, Hananiah [Shadrach], Mishael [Meshach] and Azariah [Abednego] . . ." (Daniel 1:11). On another occasion, after asking the king's officer for time to interpret Nebuchadnezzar's dream, he discussed the matter with his three friends. "He urged them to plead for mercy from the God of heaven concerning this mystery, so that he and his friends might not be executed with the rest of the wise men of Babylon" (2:18). Later Daniel was elevated to a high position, and he requested that the king appoint "Shadrach, Meshach and Abednego administrators over the province of Babylon, while Daniel himself remained at the royal court" (2:49).

King Nebuchadnezzar erected a golden statue and insisted at the sound of music that all fall down and worship the image. Shadrach, Meshach, and Abednego refused to bow and were brought to the king to be reprimanded. The king insisted they fall down and worship the image, and if they did not, they would be "thrown immediately into a blazing furnace" (3:15). They said to the king, "The God we serve is able to save us from it, and he will rescue us from your hand, O king. But even if he does not, we want you to know, O king, that we will not serve your gods or worship the image of gold you have set up" (3:17-18).

Being the only three left standing, they truly knew how to say "no" to peer pressure. Their strong commitment is seen in their reply to the king, "but even if he does not . . . we will not." Daniel's relationship with these three friends stands out. He had an influence on their saying no to Nebuchadnezzar. They learned from him; he learned from them—the four had a relationship with God and each other.

We all are an influence. What we say, how we act and conduct ourselves is seen by others. Whether we accept it or not, we are a role model that is being followed by one or more people. D. L. Moody told about a friend who met a blind man coming down the street on a very dark night with a lantern in his hand. He was surprised to see that the blind man needed the light and asked why he carried a lantern. The blind man replied, "I carry the lantern so people will not stumble over me." What a valuable lesson. May our lives not cause others to stumble.

Commitment can stand the test. "Please test your servants for ten days: Give us nothing but vegetables to eat and water to drink" (1:12). At the end of ten days, Daniel requested a comparison of "appearance with that of the young men who eat the royal food, and treat your servants in accordance with what you see" (1:13). The chief official agreed to this test and found that "at the end of the ten days they looked healthier and better nourished than any of the young men who ate the royal food" (1:15).

Daniel and his friends passed the test. It was not the vegetarian diet that caused them to pass the exam but their unwavering commitment to God regardless of the consequences. They did not shortcut or manipulate the test; it was faced with sincerity and honesty. Their commitment was pleasing to God. "When a man's ways are pleasing to the LORD, he makes even his enemies live at peace with him" (Proverbs 16:7).

God gave because Daniel was committed. "To these four young men God gave knowledge and understanding of all kinds of literature and learning. And Daniel could understand visions and dreams of all kinds" (Daniel 1:17). There is an important phrase in this verse—"God gave." God gave these four young men knowledge and understanding. He gave Daniel the ability to understand visions and dreams. Chapter 5 records the party thrown by King Belshazzar. This party was for one thousand of his nobles. Showing no respect, they drank from the goblets that Nebuchadnezzar had taken from the temple in Jerusalem.

As they drank and praised their gods, "suddenly the fingers of a human hand appeared and wrote on the plaster of the wall" (5:5). The king became frightened, and his knees knocked as he watched the hand write. Instantly he was sober at his own party. He called for the wise men of Babylon to interpret the reading. The person who could read this would become "the third highest ruler in the kingdom" (5:7).

When the queen heard that the wise men could not read the writing on the wall, she told the king about Daniel's success in interpreting dreams for Nebuchadnezzar. Daniel was summoned by the king and offered the rewards and high position as were the wise men if he could read the writing on the wall. He refused the reward and spoke with direct honesty to the king. He said he had not "humbled [him]self" (5:22). "You did not honor the God who holds in his hand your life and all your ways" (5:23).

God gave Daniel the ability to read the inscription which told of the end of the king's reign. That very evening King Belshazzar was slain. In a party of pagans, Daniel did not worry about being "politically correct" and would not compromise the truth God had shown him.

God knows all about commitment. He committed His son, Jesus Christ. "For God so loved the world that he gave his one and only Son, that whoever believes in him shall not perish but have eternal life" (John 3:16).

Commitment caused him to graduate with honors. After the test, the chief official presented Daniel and his three friends to Nebuchadnezzar. After the king talked to them, they were accepted into the king's service. He found none equal to them. "In every matter of wisdom and understanding about which the king questioned them, he found them ten times better than all the magicians and enchanters in his whole kingdom" (Daniel 1:20). Not only did these Hebrew youth pass the test, but they also passed with honors—*summa cum laude.*

Commitment is the life that lasts. "And Daniel remained there until the first year of King Cyrus" (v21). Daniel lived to be an old man. His ministry spanned through the entire Babylonian empire. During his life, he saw the whole period of Judah's captivity. His life was marked with courage, consistency, and commitment to God's Word and prayer. He lived a holy, disciplined life.

Chapter 6 captures the picture of this man's character. Daniel was one of the three administrators under King Darius. Daniel had impressed the king so much with his excellent qualities that "the king planned to set him over the whole kingdom" (v3). Being filled with jealousy, the other high government officials looked for grounds to destroy Daniel's character in the way he conducted government affairs. However, his character was so trustworthy and above reproach that they failed.

Finding no charges against him, they devised another plan. They went to the king and requested that he "issue an edict and enforce the decree that anyone who prays to any god or man during the next thirty days, except to you, O king, shall be thrown in the lions' den" (v7). The king agreed to the edict which was put in writing and could not be reversed. It was official.

When Daniel heard of the ruling, he did as was his custom. "He went home to his upstairs room where the windows opened toward Jerusalem. Three times a day he got down on his knees and prayed, giving thanks to his God, just as he had done before" (v10). The king's decree did not change Daniel's schedule. He did not panic, call the prayer chain, or call an emergency prayer meeting. He prayed and thanked God *just as he had done before.* There is no need for emergency prayer meetings if you pray everyday. The need is for consistency, consistency, and more consistency. John Wesley was asked what he would do if he knew the Lord would come at midnight tomorrow night. He replied:

> I would spend the intervening time as I intend to spend it. I would preach tonight at Glouchester and again tomorrow morning. After that I would ride to Tewkesbury, preach in the afternoon, meet the society in the evening. I should then go to Friend Martin's house as he expects to entertain me, I would converse, pray with the family, retire to my room at 10 o'clock, commend myself to my heavenly father, go sound asleep, and wake up in glory (Boyd, 25).

When the men found Daniel praying, they went to the king to report his actions. The king confirmed the decree but became very upset when he found out that Daniel was the man he had just summoned to the lions' den. He had been manipulated by his high officials. He made an effort to rescue Daniel from the ruling, but it could not be repealed. Daniel was thrown into the lions' den. The king was greatly distressed and could not sleep that night.

At the crack of dawn, the king rushed to the lions' den and called out, "Daniel, servant of the living God, has your God, whom you serve continually, been able to rescue you from the lions" (v20)? The king's question in this crisis shows the testimony of Daniel. The king saw consistency in Daniel's life—"*your God, whom you serve continually*" (emphasis added). The king had a title, but Daniel had a testimony.

Daniel responded to the king with respect. He answered, "O king, live forever! My God sent his angel, and he shut the mouths of the lions. They have not hurt me, because I was found innocent in his sight. Nor have I ever done any wrong before you, O king" (vv21-22). In these verses we see the real character of Daniel. He respected God. Although wrongly accused through manipulation by the high officials, he respected the king. He was intent on building relationships with God and one another. Instead of complaining or joining a "lion survivors group," his response was—"O king, live forever!" Spurgeon once said it was a good thing the lions did

not try to eat Daniel. They never would have enjoyed him because
he was 50 percent grit and 50 percent backbone.

Daniel was not living in a fog. He was innocent before God and
had not wronged the king. Daniel could see clearly. Not only did he
see clearly the situations of his day, but he also saw into the future
because God was with him. Daniel's life is an example of character
and consistency from which we all can learn.

Daniel is a model of consistency through changing and restless
times because he was connected to a changeless God. Although he
experienced a troubled world, he consistently followed the path of
responsibility and duty to God.

Robert Strand in his book, *Just for Fathers*, records a story I will
not soon forget:

> Surveyors were sent to a remote mountain area to map the terrain.
> Everyday they would go out over the rugged peaks and every night
> they would return to their camp. Frequently, they were joined by an
> old shepherd who enjoyed the companionship of their fire, coffee,
> and conversation. They enjoyed his company, too.
>
> One night, the old shepherd uncharacteristically insisted that he
> would accompany the surveyors the next day, so they would not
> become lost. Feeling fairly sure of themselves because they had now
> spent quite a bit of time in the mountains, they asked why he felt
> that he was needed to go along with them tomorrow.
>
> The shepherd quietly repeated, "I must go with you."
>
> Still puzzled, the surveyors again described their many hikes
> through the mountains, their up-to-date equipment, and their
> familiarity with the area after these many days. Yet, again the shep-
> herd insisted, "I know the mountains like the back of my hand."
>
> Now somewhat exasperated, the surveyors replied, "We also now
> have maps of the area which we have made."
>
> And the old shepherd responded, "But there is no fog on your
> map."

Early the next morning these two "experts" went up the mountain by themselves, to continue with their mapping. Soon a thick fog encircled them and led them astray. They wandered up and down, went in circles, growing more exhausted and more confused. Lost in the fog, they were beginning to become very frightened.

Suddenly, out of the thick fog, the shepherd appeared! And he led them safely back to camp through the fog! (16-17).

Jesus is the Good Shepherd. Let us follow Him—He will lead us through the fog of uncertainty and changing times.

References

Apthorp, Stephen P. *Alcohol and Substance Abuse.* Wilton, CT: Morehouse-Barlow, 1985.

Augsburger, David. *Caring Enough to Confront.* Glendale: Regal, 1980.

Balswick, Jack O., and Judith K. Balswick. *The Family—A Christian Perspective on the Contemporary Home.* Grand Rapids: Baker, 1989.

Barker, Joel Arthur. *Paradigms.* New York: Harper Business, 1992.

Barna, George. *Absolute Confusion.* Ventura: Regal Books, 1993.

Beattie, Melody. *Codependent No More.* New York: Harper and Row, 1988.

Benner, David G. (ed.). *Psychotherapy in Christian Perspective.* Grand Rapids: Baker, 1987.

Bennett, William J. *The Index of Leading Cultural Indicators.* New York: Simon and Schuster, 1994.

Bird, Warren. "The Great Small Group Takeover." *Christianity Today,* 7 February 1994, p. 27.

Boice, James Montgomery. *Psalms Volume I.* Grand Rapids: Baker, 1994.

Boyd, Frank M. *Pauline Epistles.* Springfield: Gospel Publishing House, 1969.

Brock, Raymond T. *Parenting the Elementary Child—Leader's Guide.* Springfield: Radiant Life, 1995.

Brownlow, Leroy. *A Time to Laugh.* Fort Worth: Brownlow Publishing Co., 1969.

Callahan, Kennon L. *Effective Church Leadership.* San Francisco: Harper and Row, 1990.

Capell-Sowder, Kathy, et al. *Codependency: An Emerging Issue.* Pompano Beach: Health Communications, 1984.

Carruth, Gorton and Eugene Ehrlich. *American Quotations.* Avenel, NJ: Outlet Book Company, 1994.

Chafer, Lewis Sperry, and John F. Walvoord. *Major Bible Themes*. Grand Rapids: Zondervan, 1974.

Collins, Gary R. *Christian Counseling*. Waco: Word, 1980.

_____. *Innovative Approaches to Counseling*. Dallas: Word, 1986.

_____, and Timothy E. Clinton. *Baby Boomer Blues*. Dallas: Word, 1992.

Colson, Charles. *The Body*. Dallas: Word, 1992.

Covey, Stephen R. *The Seven Habits of Highly Effective People*. New York: Simon and Schuster, 1989.

Crabb, Lawrence J. *Effective Biblical Counseling*. Grand Rapids: Zondervan, 1977.

Davis, John J. *Paradise to Prison*. Grand Rapids: Baker, 1975.

Elwell, Walter A. (ed.). *Evangelical Dictionary of Theology*. Grand Rapids: Baker, 1984.

George, Carl F. *The Coming Church Revolution*. Grand Rapids: Revell, 1994.

Gorman, Julie A. *Community That Is Christian*. Wheaton: Victor Books, 1993.

Halverson, Richard C. *Perspective*, Vol. XLII, No. 23, November 7, 1990, p. 1.

_____. *Perspective*, Vol. XLIII, No. 15, July 17, 1991, p. 1.

_____. *Perspective*, Vol. XLVI, No. 13, June 22, 1994, p. 1.

Hart, Archibald D. *Adrenalin and Stress*. Dallas: Word, 1991.

_____. *Counseling the Depressed*. Dallas: Word, 1987.

Hestenes, Roberta. *Using the Bible in Groups*. Philadelphia: The Westminister, 1983.

Holwerda, Jim and David Egner. "Doing Away with Addiction." *Discovery Digest*, Vol. 12, No. 4., Grand Rapids: Radio Bible Class, 1988.

Horton, Michael S. *The Law of Perfect Freedom*. Chicago: Moody Press, 1993.

Horton, Stanley M. *What the Bible Says About the Holy Spirit*. Springfield: Gospel Publishing House, 1976.

Jensen, Irving L. *Jensen's Survey of the New Testament*. Chicago: Moody Press, 1981.

Jones, E. Stanley. *Christian Maturity*. Nashville: Abingdon Press, 1957.

Johnson, Vernon E. *I'll Quit Tomorrow*. San Francisco: Harper and Row, 1980.

Krupnick, Louis B., and Elizabeth Krupnick. *From Despair to Decision*. Minneapolis: CompCare, 1985.

Kubler-Ross, Elisabeth. *On Death and Dying*. New York: Macmillan, 1970.

Kuhn, Thomas S. *The Structure of Scientific Revolutions*. Chicago: University of Chicago, 1970.

Lean, Garth. *On the Tail of a Comet*. Colorado Springs: Helmers and Howard, 1985.

Lee, Jimmy R. *Evangelism Manual*. Chattanooga: Turning Point Ministries, 1991.

_____. *Insight Group Facilitators Guide*. Chattanooga: Turning Point Ministries, 1995.

Leerhsen, Charles, and Tessa Namuth. "Alcohol and the Family." *Newsweek*, CXI, 18 January 1988, pp. 62-68.

_____. "Unite and Conquer," *Newsweek* CXV, 5 February 1990, p. 50.

Lewis, C. S. *Mere Christianity*. New York: Macmillan, 1943.

Matzat, Don. *Christ Esteem*. Eugene: Harvest House, 1990.

McGee, Robert S. *Father Hunger*. Ann Arbor: Servant Publications, 1993.

Meier, Paul D., Donald E. Ratcliff, and Frederick L. Rowe. *Child-Rearing*. Grand Rapids: Baker, 1993.

Menninger, Karl. *Whatever Became of Sin?* New York: Hawthorn, 1973.

Miller, J. Keith. *Sin: Overcoming the Ultimate Deadly Addiction*. San Francisco: Harper and Row, 1987.

Miller, Kevin Dale. "Putting an End to Christian Psychology." *Christianity Today*, 14 August 1995, p.17.

Minirth, Frank, et al. *Taking Control*. Grand Rapids: Baker, 1988.

Naisbitt, John, and Patricia Aburdene. *Megatrends 2000*. New York: Avon Books, 1990.

Narramore, S. Bruce. *No Condemnation*. Grand Rapids: Zondervan, 1984.

O'Gorman, Patricia, and Philip Oliver-Diaz. *Breaking the Cycle of Addiction*. Deerfield Beach: Health Communications, 1987.

Patterson, James, and Peter Kim. *The Day America Told the Truth*. New York: Penguin Books, 1992.

Pearlman, Myer. *Daniel Speaks Today*. Springfield: Gospel Publishing House, 1943.

Perkins, Bill. *Fatal Attractions*. Eugene: Harvest House, 1991.

Pyle, Richard. "Hoods Mimic Movie, Severely Burn Clerk." *Chattanooga Free Press*, 27 November 1995, p. A1.

Raspberry, William. "The Real Work of the Church." *The Chattanooga Times*, 13 February 1995, p. A2.

Resnik, Hank (ed.). *Youth and Drugs: Society's Mixed Messages*. Rockville: U. S. Department of Health and Human Services, 1990.

Seamands, David A. *Healing for Damaged Emotions*. Wheaton: Victor Books, 1981.

Stanley, Charles F. *Handle with Care*. Wheaton: Victor, 1988.

Sweeten, Gary R. *Apples of Gold II Teacher's Manual*. Cincinnati: Christian Information Committee, 1983.

Stott, John. *The Gospel and the End of Time*. Downers Grove: InterVarsity, 1991.

Strand, Robert. *Just for Fathers*, Springfield: Access, 1994.

Tan, Paul Lee. *Encyclopedia of 7700 Illustrations*. Rockville: Assurance Publisher, 1979.

ten Boom, Corrie. *The Hiding Place*. New York: Bantam Books, 1974.

Tenny, Merrill C. *New Testament Times*. Grand Rapids: Eerdmans, 1965.

Toffler, Alvin. *Power Shift*. New York: Bantam Books, 1991.

Turnbull, Ralph G. (ed.). *Baker's Handbook of Practical Theology*. Grand Rapids: Baker, 1967.

Twerski, Abraham. *Addictive Thinking*. New York: Harper and Row, 1990.

VanVonderen, Jeffrey. *Good News for the Chemically Dependent*. Nashville: Thomas Nelson, 1985.

Wuthnow, Robert. "How Small Groups Are Transforming Our Lives." *Christianity Today*, 7 February 1994, pp. 23-24.